CLEVELAND TV

Memories

Tom Feran and R. D. Heldenfels

GRAY & COMPANY, PUBLISHERS • CLEVELAND

Library of Congress Cataloging-in-Publication Data
Feran, Tom.
Cleveland TV memories / by Tom Feran and R.D. Heldenfels.
1. Television broadcasting—Ohio—Cleveland—Miscellanea.
I. Heldenfels, R. D. (Richard D.) II. Title.
PN1992.3.U5F47 1999   791.45'09771'32--dc21
99-6827 CIP

Gray & Company, Publishers
1588 E. 40th Street, Cleveland, Ohio 44103
www.grayco.com

ISBN 1-886228-35-3

Printed in the United States of America
10 9 8 7 6 5 4 3 2 1

"Clevelanders are a great audience. They do not like change. They like something to be around forever."
—"Big Chuck" Schodowski

"Everybody likes to see themselves on television."
—Don Webster

Acknowledgments

We would like to extend special thanks to the *Cleveland Press* Collection at the Cleveland State University Archives for permission to reproduce various pictures, and to Bill Becker and the staff of CSU for their generous research assistance.

Thanks also to Gary Stark, program and research director of WEWS, for providing access to station archives and permission to reproduce pictures, as well as for his unsurpassed memory and good will. Similar grateful acknowledgment goes to Kevin Salyer, director of programming and promotion for WJW, and to Peg Neeson and her staff at WVIZ.

We also thank everyone who shared TV memories and provided assistance, most notably, Dave Howitt, Chuck Schodowski, Ralph Tarsitano, Bob Ferguson, P.J. Bednarski, Dave Little, Joanne Stern, Dale Kirk, Bob Seeley, Jim Pockmire, Tom Sr. and Adeline Feran, Sandy Kish Jordan, Rich O'Dell, and the incomparable library staffs of The *Plain Dealer* and the *Akron Beacon Journal*.

Finally, we extend thanks and acknowledgment for pain and suffering to our family members: Amy, Meghan, Spencer, Christopher and Caroline, and Brendan and Conor.

Introduction

This book is for the people who think of Tim Taylor as a surrogate father, Fred Griffith as a kindly uncle, Robin Swoboda as a neighbor who stirred previously unarticulated feelings, and Barnaby as better than any imaginary friend you could come up with your own. These are flashes from the first half-century of Cleveland television—from the days when you could only get one channel on a black-and-white set, to today's home theater system bearing as many channels as your wallet can afford.

These are your individual memories and our collective consciousness: a name, a word, or a phrase is sometimes all it takes to bring back a whole era or a specific day of our lives: the time you got Captain Penny's autograph at Kenny King's; the day you met Big Wilson at the Boat Show; the afternoon you saw Ghoulardi at Euclid Beach Park; the nights you rushed home to watch your high school game replayed on Channel 25. Good times and sad times, too. We remember because we have to.

Because, no matter what our differences, we are all members of the Grand and Exalted Lodge of TV Viewers. Its grand poobah is handsome downstairs neighbor Jerry Kriegle. Its phone number is GArfield 1-2323.

Its headquarters is in our hearts.

1. **Booth announcers** were heard but not seen as they delivered live station identifications and program times in the years before tape, satellite, and computer technology made the job obsolete. Many of them also appeared on commercials or as program hosts. Channel 3's Tom Haley was the last of the breed. Among others well-remembered locally: Howard Hoffman, Ernie Anderson, Ron Penfound, Paul Bedford, and Court Stanton.

2. **The Clean Plate Club** kept no official roster, but you were a member if you ate your whole lunch while watching Captain Penny.

3. **"Readings by Robert"** was a *Hoolihan & Big Chuck* feature borrowed from the Percy Dovetonsils character of Ernie Kovacs. Bob "Hoolihan" Wells lisped bad poetry while sitting in a wing chair, wearing google-eye glasses and a smoking jacket.

4. *Remember when* stations used "Indian Head" test patterns to measure the resolution, or sharpness, of their signals? Lines in the vertical and horizontal parts of a cross framing "The Chief of the Airwaves" got narrower as they reached the center of the picture, turning to gray hash as the limits of resolution were reached. The Indian's headdress also tested resolution: if feather details were clearly visible, engineers had a good adjustment.

5. **Network Ties Didn't Bind:** WJW was affiliated with the struggling DuMont network when it signed on the air as WXEL (Channel 9) in 1949. WJW switched to CBS in January 1956 through the intercession of then-owner Storer Broadcasting.

6. **Og the Leprechaun** from *Finian's Rainbow* was the inspiration for TV-3's Barnaby a decade later. Linn Sheldon used mortician's wax for a pointy-eared effect.

7. **Joe Howard and his band**—pianist Joe Howard, a drummer, and bassist—provided the music on the *1 O'Clock Club*. Howard also provided the theme for Captain Penny's *Funny Fun Fun Train*.

Courtesy of Channel 5

8. **Pilot Error:** Cleveland references and landmarks abound on *The Drew Carey Show*, usually with dead-on accuracy, but its pilot episode had one slip-up: a reference to the "diamond lane" for car pools. They're found in southern California, but not Cleveland.

9. **The great blizzard of November 1950** gave WEWS, less than two years old, a chance to show TV's public-service potential by discarding its regular schedule for round-the-clock coverage. Betty Cope, who started as a station receptionist but became the first female producer-director, rode into local legend by traveling to work on horseback over otherwise impassable roads.

Paige Palmer and Betty Cope, 1957

10. Most Clevelanders needed **set-top converters** with an extra dial if they wanted to watch WVIZ when it began service as "educational television" on Channel 25 in 1965. It was Cleveland's first ultra-high frequency station, and TV sets manufactured before 1963 were not required to receive the UHF signals above channel 13.

11. **The Early Bird Gets The Audience**: When KYW launched *The Mike Douglas Show* in 1961, it started at 12:55 p.m. daily to get a five-minute jump on the *1 O'Clock Club* on WEWS.

12. **The K That Came And Went**: WJW-TV had to use the call letters WJKW for nearly a decade, starting in 1977, after the sale of its sister radio station that had original claim to the name. When the radio station was sold again and became WRMR, Channel 8 jumped at the chance to reclaim the distinctive three-letter identification—though an outline of the K remained visible long after it was removed from TV-8's building beside the Shoreway.

Cleveland **TV** Memories

Channel 8 logo, first used in 1957.

13. *Signature Saying:* Mike Massa, a Cleveland public schools teacher and principal, started as a volunteer at WVIZ (Channel 25) and became its sports director, announcing high school football, basketball, and wrestling in the 1970s. He ended each telecast saying, "Have a great sports weekend!"

14. **The "1 O'Clock Club"** really did resemble a club. Instead of bleacher seats, its studio audience sat at white-cloth-covered tables sipping coffee and finishing a meal. Cost of the pre-show luncheon in 1958 was $1.50.

15. **"The Arthur Murray Show,"** hosted by Jean Hughes and Del Torto, offered Sunday afternoon music and dance instruction in the late 1950s on Channel 8.

16. **Randy Culver**—sometimes in choir robes—was the dark-haired booth announcer and tenor who sang as the "vocalist" on the *1 O'Clock Club*.

17. **"Weekday Fever"** was Channel 3's gift to would-be
Travoltas, launched in September 1978 as "the
nation's first locally produced five-day-a-week
show devoted entirely to disco." Most of the show
was shot in the Nite Moves disco in The Flats. Co-
hosts were local deejay Tim Byrd and Nanci
Glass, later famous as host of the news magazine
American Journal, but then a 24-year-old writer, producer, and TV personality who was also co-hosting Channel 3's weekday morning show "Zap,"
with Bob Zappe.

18. **Joe Bova** was the bowler-hatted young kiddie host known as "Uncle Joe"
on shows like *Noontime Comics* and *Tip Top Comics* on old WNBK. He left
Cleveland in 1955 for stage acting and commercial work in New York.

19. In the late 1960s, Northeast Ohio awaited the start of a new station when TV evangelist **Rex Humbard** got a license to go on the air and erected a tower for broadcast facilities in Cuyahoga Falls at his Cathedral of Tomorrow—in whose honor he planned to call the station WCOT. Lack of funds killed the idea. Humbard's facilities were sold to another evangelist, Ernest Angley, who used them to launch WBNX (Channel 55). Its call sign includes the initials for owner Winston Broadcasting Network.

20. **"The Prize Movie,"** offering viewers a call-for-cash jackpot, appeared on Channel 43 early on weekday afternoons. Outspoken morning personality John Lanigan of WGAR-AM—then sporting a mustache and corona of curly hair—hosted it from 1975 to 1984, when he left for a job in Tampa. David "Fig" Newton of WWWE-AM took over until Lanigan returned to town at WMJI-FM in late 1985. *The Prize Movie* was canceled in 1993, and Lanigan was told he'd get another TV show—which turned out to be *The Prize Movie*, reappearing briefly the following year.

21. *And now, a word from our sponsor:* "Chevy, Chevy,/See Commander Ray/At West Park Chevrolet." Set to the tune "Sailin' Sailin'" in commercials that started appearing in the early 1960s, the jingle was accompanied by the cartoon of a saluting "Commander Ray" Herzberger. An Annapolis graduate and former navy pilot, he resigned from the service with the rank of commander in 1954 to help run West Park Chevrolet, the dealership founded by his father in 1927. He retired from running the business in 1986 and died in March 1998.

22. *Signature Saying:* Linn Sheldon closed every show as Barnaby by telling the "little neighbors" in his audience, "If anybody calls, tell 'em Barnaby says hello. And tell them I said you're the nicest person in the world. Just you."

23. **"ei8ht Is News"** was the ubiquitous and relentlessly repeated slogan that became a mantra for WJW in late 1995. One of the most effective TV image campaigns ever to hit town, it restored the old practice from the 60s and 70s of using the numerical "8" for the lower-case "g" in the station's logo and was later dropped for "Fox 8."

24. **Blanche Arbriton** was the pianist and music director for the singers and dancers on *The Gene Carroll Show*.

25. **Price and Pride** was the last-ditch TV campaign that A&P supermarkets hoped would increase their share of the local grocery market. Pitchman "Price" was a spectacled, pecunious-looking grocer in a white apron who promised value as he stood beside beefy, gregarious "Pride," who promised quality.

26. **Sam Sheppard,** who was convicted, retried, and acquitted of the murder of his wife, Marilyn, in Cleveland's most famous criminal case, was played by George Peppard in the three-hour movie *Guilty or Innocent: The Sam Sheppard Murder Case* in November 1975. Twenty-three years later—to the day—Peter Strauss played Dr. Sam in the two-hour *My Father's Shadow: The Sam Sheppard Story*, based on a book co-authored by Sheppard's son, Sam Reese Sheppard, who was played by Henry Czerny. The subject of both movies saw neither one: he died in 1970.

27. Not only a commentator, reviewer, and interviewer, **Dorothy Fuldheim** was the author of four books: the memoirs *A Thousand Friends* (Doubleday, 1974) and *I Laughed, I Cried, I Loved* (World, 1966), the semi-autobiographical novel *Three and a Half Husbands* (Simon & Schuster, 1976), and a collection of her observations after the Six-Day War, *Where Were the Arabs?* (World, 1967).

28. Disc jockey **Ken "Super K" Hawkins** of WJMO radio hosted *The Big K World of Soul*, a local version of *Soul Train* that appeared late on Friday nights in 1968 on Channel 5. Hawk featured music that put "the hop in your hoof, the dip in your hip, the cut in your strut, and the glide in your stride—and if you can't dig it, uh huh, you got a great big hole in your soul."

29. **"The Friedman Buick Dance Party"** appeared on Saturday mornings for 82 weeks on Channel 5 in the late 1950s. It was hosted by Norman Wain, who was previously a disc jockey on WDOK, then an advertising executive, and later an owner of fabled WIXY radio.

30. **The Woollybear Festival** was started by Channel 8 meteorologist and folklorist Dick Goddard as a wacky event devoted to the weather-forecasting woollybear caterpillar. The first was held in October 1973 in Birmingham, Ohio. Too large for the small town after eight years, the event moved to Vermilion and became Ohio's largest single-day festival.

31. **Pete "Mad Daddy" Myers** was probably the shortest-tenured horror movie host in local history. No records even exist of how long Myers, a wild, rhyming deejay on WJW and later WHK radio, plied his strange act on Channel 8 in early 1958. But fans remember his "wavy gravy" hipster patter, his on-camera tricks (such as broadcasting his image upside down) and his hooded velvet "nightmare robe." It set the tone for Ghoulardi five years later.

32. **"The Cleveland News,"** which ended publication in January 1960, featured exhaustive coverage of TV by writers Maurice Van Metre and Bert J. Reesing.

33. **"The Dave Patterson Show"** was the predecessor of *AM Cleveland* on Channel 3. Host Dave Patterson, who had jumped to the station from co-anchoring *Eyewitness News* on Channel 5, gave it up to return to full-time news duties at a station in Arizona.

34. **STAR LOG, I.** National TV looks a lot like Northeast Ohio when you consider the local folk who've gone on to wider fame. Among them: Roger Ailes (Fox News president), Ernie Anderson (the voice of ABC), writer-producer Tom Anderson (*Living Single*), Kaye Ballard (*The Mothers-in-Law*), Halle Berry (*Introducing Dorothy Dandridge*, where Berry played Cleveland's Dandridge), John Beradino (*General Hospital*), David Birney (*St. Elsewhere*), James Black (*The Burning Zone*), MTV veejay Nina Blackwood, Danny Breen (*Not Necessarily the News*), writer-producers Andy Borowitz (*Fresh Prince of Bel Air*) and Brannon Braga (*Star Trek: Voyager*), writer-actor James Brogan (*The Tonight Show*), Richard Brooks (*Law & Order*), Drew Carey (*The Drew Carey Show*). . .

35. **And She Plays One On TV:** Years before she moved from Channel 43 to Channel 3, news anchor Romona Robinson jumped to Channel 5—just for one night in March of 1992. She played Melanie Scott, a hard-charging TV reporter at the scene of a big fire in an episode of ABC's *The Commish*. Robinson had once told Stephen J. Cannell, whose studio owned Channel 43 and produced *The Commish*, that she fantasized about playing a TV reporter on *Hunter*.

36. Former Indians pitcher **Jim "Mudcat" Grant** kept viewers and TV announcing partner Harry Jones entertained and astonished during less-than-stellar Tribe games from 1973 to 1977. Besides genially butchering the names of players and cities (Bucyrus, Ohio, was variously rendered as "Book-a-rus" or "Bussy-rus"), "Mud" sent greetings to favored "ladies" among the fans and once offered his advice for a tough pitching situation: "I'd throw the spitter, Harry—like lightning."

37. **Anchors Ago:** The local news teams of 1975, midway through the first half-century of Cleveland television, included some anchors from the 1950s and others who would last into the 21st century. Here's who was on the air, 25 years ago: *Action 3 News* had anchors Doug Adair and Mike Landess with Russ Montgomery (weather) and Jim Graner (sports); Channel 5's *Eyewitness News* featured Ted Henry and Dave Patterson with Don Webster (weather) and Gib Shanley (sports); and Channel 8's *City Camera* had Jeff Maynor and Jim Hale with Dick Goddard (weather) and Jim Mueller (sports).

38. Some of the items blown up by **The Ghoul** on Saturday night on Channel 61 show: "Froggy" (a plastic frog doll and regular sketch character on the show), kielbasi, pizza, model cars, carp, cheeze whiz, turkeys, soup cans, garbage cans, pierogies, toilets, film reels, LP records, shirts, viewer mail, guitars, model airplanes, Mickey Mouse, Beatles figurines, televisions, model boats, radios, skulls, arts and crafts, 45 records, 5-quart containers of strawberries, flared pants, and the back of a fan's Levi's.

39. Despite default and financial crisis, **Mayor Dennis Kucinich** found time to feud with local TV stations in 1978. He blasted WEWS and WJW for not carrying a potentially libelous ad opposing the sale of the Muny Light system. Then, he complained to the FCC after the stations refused to televise his planned speech on the financial crisis. The stations made counter-offers, such as including Kucinich in part of a panel discussing the issue, but he turned them down.

40. **The Glass Harp**, a hot Ohio band of the early "progressive" era led by guitar wizard Phil Keaggy, was the big attraction in 1972 when Channel 25 teamed with WMMS-FM for what they billed as the nation's first TV-radio simulcast.

41. Jane Fonda joined husband Ted Turner, owner of the Atlanta Braves, taunting Cleveland fans with **the "tomahawk chop"** during the 1995 World Series—a duel of politically incorrect team names logos and mascots.

42. Canton native **Jack Paar** was once a Cleveland radio personality—the on-duty announcer at WGAR the night of Orson Welles' infamous "War of the Worlds" broadcast—before succeeding Steve Allen as host of the *The Tonight Show* in 1957. Paar, king of late-night until 1962, described the difference between being born in Canton, Ohio, and Canton, China, in his 1960 memoir, *I Kid You Not*: "If it had been China and not Ohio, I might still be on television but, considering the history of Orientals in show business, I'd probably be juggling instead of just talking."

43. **Spice Guy:** Singer Terry Knight, of Terry Knight and the Pack, explained to Don Webster on *Upbeat* that he got lost in the east suburbs because he was confused by Shaker Heights and Pepper Pike. Since pepper comes out of a shaker, he figured "Pepper Pike" was just a nickname for Shaker.

44. *Remember when* Gary Short used a good-night wink to end the brief nightly *Update* that ran on Channel 43 before it started *The Ten O'Clock News*?

45. Great players and great announcers have been among the **Tribe's TV announcers,** and fans well know the current longtime teams: Jack Corrigan and Mike Hegan on WUAB and Rick Manning and John Sanders on cable's Fox Sports Ohio. Other voices since 1948: Jack Graney, Jimmy Dudley, Hal Newell, Bob Neal, Red Jones, Ken Coleman, Jim Britt, Bill McColgan, Rocky Colavito, Jim "Mudcat" Grant, Bob Brown, Jim Mueller, Eddie Doucette, Joe Castiglione, Fred McLeon, Joe Tait, Bruce Drennan, Bob Feller, Denny Schreiner, Reggie Rucker, and Steve Lamar.

Joe Tipton (left) and Bob Neal, 1957

46. **Carl Reese**, best known as a radio announcer since the 1950s, was on WERE when he started hosting TV's late-night *Action Theater* on Channel 5, and on WJW's *Caravan* when he appeared in spots for Star Muffler.

47. Cleveland's first half-hour newscast, **"Eyewitness News,"** debuted in 1959 on KYW (Channel 3) and was anchored by Carl Stern and Bud Dancy.

Channel 3 anchor team, 1961

48. **Howard Hoffmann** became familiar to viewers from 37 years as a weatherman and announcer on Channel 8. He was the original booth announcer who signed on with WXEL (Channel 9) in 1949 after joining the station from WHK radio, and also had network credits: he was one of the original singing "Men from Texaco" on the *Texaco Star Theater* with Milton Berle, and traveled as a vocalist with the Stan Kenton band.

49. "The male seat" on *CBS 19 News* was occupied by a woman, **Gretchen Carlson,** when the station paired her with Denise Dufala as Cleveland's first regularly scheduled week night two-woman anchor team from April 1996 to December 1997. Dufala kept "the female seat." The team was disbanded when Carlson was canned because, a station executive said, Clevelanders "did not want to see a dual female anchor team. They want a more traditional male-female anchor team."

50. **King Jack** wore silvery-looking royal robes and a crown—of course—to host *King Jack's Toybox*, the afternoon kids' show that was popular on old WXEL in the early 1950s.

Pat Ryan Dopp, King Jack (Bogo Heath) and Jester, Wally Sanford, 1957

Dick Goddard

51. Wally Kinnan the Weatherman was the jovial, pipe-smoking, trumpet-playing meteorologist who replaced **Dick Goddard** on Channel 3 in 1965, after the federal government ordered NBC and Westinghouse to undo their 10-year-old station swap and Goddard went to Philadelphia with KYW and Westinghouse. When Goddard, who already was called by *The Plain Dealer* "perhaps the most popular weatherman ever to appear on television here," immediately wanted to return, every station in town wooed him. The 35-year-old meteorologist said he picked WJW "because they had the Browns games."

52. **Nose For News:** A "funniest video" of Channel 8 was recorded in the 1980s when a station employee's pet Labrador retriever wandered onto the news set while Mark Koontz was delivering the weather—and stuck its nose in his crotch. The dog's name, for the record, was Oscar.

53. **Tackling Hollywood:** Euclid's Bob Golic moved closer to the cameras in 1993, after ending an NFL career that had taken him from the Browns and Cleveland to the Raiders and Los Angeles in 1989. He played a former football player with steroid-induced cancer on ABC's *Coach*, a football player nicknamed Scud on CBS's *Good Advice* with Shelley Long, and then became a regular as a dorm adviser on NBC's *Saved By the Bell: The College Years*.

54. **Larry, Curly, and Moe** is the way you refer to the Three Stooges—if you're from Cleveland. The order was favored by Ron "Captain Penny" Penfound, and stood in contrast to "Moe, Larry, and Curly," the order in most other places. TV critic and Cleveland native P.J. Bednarski remembers being shocked when he wrote about "Larry, Curly, and Moe" in *USA Today*, and the copy editors changed it.

55. **Skeeter Scarecrow** was the somewhat-frightening looking character played by Janet Horn Sonneborn on *Uncle Ed's Magic Farm*, sponsored by Weather-Bird Shoes from 1948–1950 on Channel 5.

56. **Otis Redding** made his final TV appearance in December 1967 on Channel 5's *Upbeat* show, singing "Respect," "Try a Little Tenderness" and—in duet with Mitch Ryder—"Knock on Wood." Later that night, on his way from Cleveland to Wisconsin, the legendary singer-songwriter, just 26 years old, was killed in a plane crash with four members of his band.

57. **Big-Time Wrestling:** Professional wrestlers came to town for weekly TV shows in the 1960s. Fans at home watched Bobo Brazil administer his "cocoa butt" head bop; saw The Sheik blind opponents with a flame that "might" have come from a huge and conspicuous bandage on his hand; listened to Wild Bull Curry growl; heard Thunderbolt Patterson disdain rematches with the villains he beat with flying dropkicks because, "I don't want to get sweat in my threads," and waited for the novelty of lady wrestlers, midget wrestlers, and 600-pound Happy Humphrey.

58. **TV's "Play Lady"** wore a billowing, festive skirt, kept kids busy with games and activities on Channel 8 and Channel 5, and teamed up at the holidays with Mr. Jingeling. Her real name was Pat Ryan Dopp.

"Play Lady" Pat Dopp, Archibald Frog and Mr. Banjo, 1957

Courtesy of Channel 8

59. **Tale of the Tape:** "Big Chuck" Schodowski stands 6 feet 2 inches tall. "Lil' John" Rinaldi stands 4 foot 3.

60. **Franz the Toymaker** really knew how to use a hammer. The Channel 8 kids' host of the mid-sixties was Ray Stawiarski, who did carpentry—including building sets for a Columbus TV station—before teaching children how to make their own toys in Columbus and then Cleveland. He had a simple way of making sure tots at home could make the toys: his own three children tried his ideas first.

61. *Signature Saying:* Bob Wells, the Channel 8 forecaster who was better known as Hoolihan the Weatherman, ended his segments wishing viewers, "Sunshine to ya!"

62. **"Big Ginger"** was the soft-drink equivalent of "Hey Mabel." She was the winking, bubbly blonde who appeared on commercials for—what else?—ginger ale, in big 2-liter containers, from Cleveland's Cotton Club Bottling Company.

63. Square-jawed, plummy-voiced, and peering through horn-rimmed glasses, **Seth "Tom" Field** was one of Cleveland's favorite early news anchors. Originally heard on WTAM radio, he moved to TV on WNBK, moved with NBC in 1955 to Philadelphia, and returned to Cleveland on WEWS in 1961. He ended his career as a newscaster on old WDBN, an FM easy-listening station.

Dorothy Fuldheim and Tom Field, 1958

64. **How's That Again?** Dick Goddard meant to tell viewers about the meteorological significance of croaking frogs when he referred to "froaking crogs" in his first forecast on TV-3 in May 1961. It was the first of his verbal somersaults known as "spoonerisms." More recently, he predicted a "cold mare's ass" was on its way from Canada, and announced that Channel 8's portion of the 21st annual *Jerry Lewis MDA Telethon* was coming live from "beautiful Stouffer's Sour Titty Plaza!"

65. **Shapely Paige Palmer** donned a leotard to battle the scourge of "saddlebag thighs" with "fanny bumps" on her morning exercise and beauty show, *The Paige Palmer Show*, on WEWS. Palmer, a native of Akron, ran her own dance studio and later worked in New York with cosmetics queen Helena Rubenstein. Palmer hosted the first "women's show" on WEWS in 1947, manufactured her own exercise equipment, designed her own line of leotards, and was named to the President's Committee for Physical Fitness in 1962. After developing Meniere's Disease, which affects balance and hearing, she left TV in 1973 and became a travel writer.

Paige Palmer at work, with Nancy Gallagher and Bill "Dad" Wiedenmann, 1957.

66. *Remember when* TV weathermen wore station-attendant shirts from sponsoring oil companies like Atlantic and Phillips 66?

67. **Gone Too Soon:** Credible and neighborly, Martin Ross and Murray Stewart became one of Cleveland's most popular anchor teams ever, after they were paired on Channel 8's *City Camera News* in 1970. Tragedy struck only three years later: Ross died of cancer in April 1973 and Stewart, suffering a glandular illness, switched to reduced duties off the evening news soon after, and took his own life in August 1976.

68. *Remember when* weathermen displayed their maps on blackboards and then on sliding panels, before "blue screen" equipment permitted the maps to be shown electronically behind them?

69. *Signature Saying:* Warren Guthrie, the Case Western Reserve University speech instructor who delivered the news as "The Sohio Reporter" on Channel 8 from 1951 to 1963, closed his late-evening broadcasts saying, "Sohio everyone!"

70. **STAR LOG, II.** More Northeast Ohio folk who've gone on to national TV fame: Nancy Cartwright (the voice of Bart Simpson), Vince Cellini (CNN), Bill Cobbs (*Decoration Day*), Townsend Coleman (*Teenage Mutant Ninja Turtles*), NBC tennis guru Bud Collins, Tim Conway (*The Carol Burnett Show*), horrormeister Wes Craven (*Nightmare Cafe*), Jim Cummings (Disney cartoons), NBC correspondent John "Bud" Dancy, Frank Dicopoulos (*Guiding Light*), Dan Dierdorf (CBS football analyst), Phyllis Diller (*The Beautiful Phyllis Diller Show*), Denny Dillon (*Dream On*), NBC correspondent Tom Donovan, talk-show host Mike Douglas, Hugh Downs (*20/20*), writer-performer Ann Elder (*Laugh-In*) . . .

71. **"Hey, Mister Banjo, play a song for me!"** That was the song in the 1950s for Channel 8's Mister Banjo (Davy Herbert), distinctively clad in a vest, bowtie, and bowler hat.

72. **"The Carnival Kickback Trial"** of 1979 found eight sitting and former Cleveland City Council members in court on charges—all eventually dismissed—of bribery, theft in office, and extortion, for their role in getting permits for carnival operators. Interest ran so high that the trial was televised by Channel 25 as the first and only gavel-to-gavel TV coverage of a trial in Ohio.

73. **"Frank & Drac"** were comical versions of Frankenstein and Dracula, played respectively by Alan Christopher and Bob Kokai, during their brief stint as late-night movie hosts on Channel 19 at the end of the eighties. Kokai's dead-on Humphrey Bogart impression also made him familiar as a detective in skits on *The Big Chuck & Lil' John Show* on Channel 8.

74. **"Pooch Parade"** is most remembered as the segment on *Captain Penny's Fun House* featuring dogs and cats up for adoption from the Animal Protective League. But it started earlier in the '50s as a popular short program of its own hosted by Bob Dale and Freda Champion.

75. **George Anthony Moore** worked at WEWS as one of TV's first African-American producer-directors. Later a *Cleveland Press* columnist and public relations specialist, he became familiar to viewers as host of the Sunday morning *Ebony Showcase* in the late 1950s.

76. **"Pepski"** was the soft drink in a favorite *Big Chuck & Lil' John* skit. "Nice can," John remarks, after Chuck purchases the newly repacked product from a vending machine—only to get clobbered by a passing woman who takes his comment personally.

77. *Signature Saying:* The daily payoff on Channel 5's *Romper Room* came when "Miss Barbara" Plummer looked into the camera, held her "magic mirror" before her face and said: "Romper stomper bomper boo/Tell me, tell me, tell me do/Magic mirror, tell me today/Have all my friends had fun at play?" A kaleidoscope distracted viewers while she switched from a hand mirror to one missing the glass—so she could "see" them right through it.

"Miss Barbara" on Romper Room

78. **"Wahoo, What a Finish,"** a home video produced by SportsChannel, highlighted the Tribe's 1995 season heroics and the late-inning lightning at Jacobs Field.

79. **The first "Monday Night Football" game** was played in Cleveland on September 21, 1970, when the Browns beat the Jets, 31-21. National TV ratings proved that the telecasts could succeed—as Browns owner Art Modell had argued—and the attendance of 85,073 at Cleveland Stadium set a Browns record. Other local fans had to listen on the radio—the game was blacked out in Cleveland.

80. **Getting Their Perps:** Fox's *Cops* hit Cleveland in the summer of 1993 for a memorable series of shows first seen that November. "We've covered many car chases and pursuits, and we've never seen as many successfully concluded in any other city as we had in Cleveland," gushed executive producer Malcolm Barbour. "It seemed every time they take off after a car, they catch the guy."

81. **Not the Nicest:** Linn "Barnaby" Sheldon liked to assure his TV fans that each was "the nicest person in the world." An exception was a tough, stocky kid at a personal appearance who asked if Sheldon really thought that. When Sheldon said yes and bent down to grant the youngster's request for a hug, the kid beaned Sheldon with a ketchup bottle, leaving him in need of 18 stitches. Barnaby wore a toupee to cover the injury.

82. **A prancing zebra** became the unofficial mascot and symbol of public station WVIZ after its founding general manager, Betty Cope, quipped that its call letters stood for "Very Important Zebras." They actually stand for "viz.," from the Latin "videlicet," meaning "one may see," or "that is." Cope made her off-the-cuff zebra joke when, addressing to a group, she saw their eyes glaze over during the real definition.

83. **Final View:** On Friday, July 27, 1984, Dorothy Fuldheim taped a satellite interview with President Ronald Reagan and delivered a commentary for the 6 p.m. news on WEWS before she was felled by a blood clot to the brain. She never returned to the air after surgery and a series of strokes, but lived until the age of 96 and died on November 3, 1989.

84. Wrestling fans of the 1950s and early '60s always waited for suave but hulking announcer **Lord Layton** to doff his continental suit and tie and thrash some manners into the ring's unruly villains, who often asked for it by busting up Layton's flimsy ringside announcing desk and trying to blind-side him with a wooden folding chair.

85. **Book reviews delivered by Dorothy Fuldheim** from a wing-back chair turned into dramatic performances that enthralled audiences on the *1 O'Clock Club*, where other regular segments included "Expert's Corner" and "Community Talent Spotlight."

86. **Sign of Spring:** No matter what the calendar says, since 1968, spring arrives on Cleveland TV with WVIZ's annual on-air auction. Banks of volunteers take phoned-in bids from viewers while station staffers and local celebrities act as auctioneers for everything from small household items to luxury vacations and cars. Buzzers, bells and sirens fill the air and a jamboree atmosphere enlivens the station into the wee hours for more than a week.

87. *And now, a word from our sponsor:* "Yoo hoo—Mabel? Black Label! Carling Black Label beer!" advertised Cleveland's Carling Brewing Company until the Mabel character was retired in 1965. The company then started touting "The Carling Philosophy," which looked like the Magna Carta and basically promised fresh beer.

88. **The Rock and Roll Hall of Fame and Museum** opened on Labor Day Weekend 1995, highlighted by a seven-hour inaugural concert telecast on HBO that began full restoration of Cleveland's national image and might have been the last great event at Cleveland Stadium. A local highlight found Akron's Chrissie Hynde of the Pretenders greeting the crowd with "What about that Tribe?" She then recited a list of local communities—Akron, Ashtabula, Berea, Cleveland, Canton, Kent, Barberton, Sharon, Zanesville, Hartville, Seneca, and Warrensville—before singing her "back to Ohio" lament, "My City Was Gone."

89. **The Cleveland Challenge:** After Cleveland's national image took a beating in the late 1970s, and after the recession of 1982, Channel 3 launched a campaign to save itself—trying to buff its image for the home crowd with "The Cleveland Challenge," which had anchor Judd Hambrick comparing life in other major cities to the North Coast in areas like recreation, arts, and transit.

90. *Signature Saying:* On Channel 3 and later on Channel 5, Bill Jorgensen ended his newscasts by "thanking you for your time, this time . . . until next time."

91. **Carmel Quinn** was the first guest co-host of *The Mike Douglas Show*. Heavy promotion of the Irish singer's week-long appearance gave her an indelible association with the show.

92. **Traffic lights** hanging over Euclid Avenue prevent the use of Macy's Parade-style balloons, but waves of marching bands, entertainers and floats galore distinguish the annual "TV-8/American Legion Christmas Parade" in downtown Cleveland. TV-8 has been staging and broadcasting the parade live on the Saturday morning after Thanksgiving since 1985.

93. **"Matty's Funday Funnies"** was TV's one oasis for kids on Sunday after-noon when it debuted in 1960. Sponsored by Mattel, it soon became *Beany and Cecil.*

94. **Change of Scene:** Motorists who passed Channel 25's headquarters at 4300 Brookpark Road into the 1960s remember that the building—now studded with antennas and satellite dishes—used to be a tractor factory. Its high ceilings made it easy to convert into studios.

95. **Cleveland's first 10 p.m. newscast** debuted on WKBF Channel 61 in August 1968, anchored by John Herrington and using the slogan "An Hour Ahead of the Pack." Hampered by a small staff and thin commercial sup-port, it had its final broadcast on November 12, 1970.

96. **Longjohn** was Barnaby's invisible parrot. He sometimes "perched" on Barnaby's shoulder, but otherwise occupied an apparently empty cage—while Linn Sheldon used his skill at ventriloquism to supply the parrot's squawks and voice. He also had a butterfly named Cicero sumperimposed on the television screen.

97. **"Martha in the Middle"** was what they called the half-hour Martha Stewart show that oddly ran in the middle of the two-hour *Morning Exchange* in 1997. Channel 5 had no other place for the Stewart show, which it was compelled to carry by a syndication agreement, and *Morning Exchange* was in a retooling, which began after it was moved from its familiar 8 a.m. slot to make way for *Good Morning America* in September 1994.

98. Channel 5 also operated a radio station, **NEWS-FM,** when it first signed on the air. The radio station, at 102.1 mHz, was sold in 1950 and became WDOK-FM.

99. **Paul Sciria** looked like a cop and had the hoarse, streetwise sound of a guy-in-the-know as he patrolled the city in a radio car as Channel 3's first street reporter, starting at the end of the 1950s.

100. **Andrea Carroll** (real name: Andrea DeCapite) was one of the biggest stars

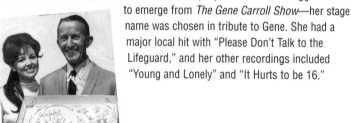

to emerge from *The Gene Carroll Show*—her stage name was chosen in tribute to Gene. She had a major local hit with "Please Don't Talk to the Lifeguard," and her other recordings included "Young and Lonely" and "It Hurts to be 16."

101. **Country singer Dottie West**—later famous for the jingle and single "Country Sunshine"—began crooning for Clevelanders in 1954 on Channel 5's Saturday evening music series *Landmark Jamboree* with her then-husband, Bill West. She continued for a year with the show, which was hosted by WERE deejay Tommy Edwards and sponsored by the Farm Bureau.

102. **Channel 8** started service in Parma in a gleaming building at Pleasant Valley and State roads that was built for WXEL. It relocated to the former Lake Theater, a Georgian brick building on the south side of Euclid Avenue at East 17th Street off Playhouse Square, before moving to quarters off the Shoreway on the South Marginal Road near East 55th Street.

103. **Crandall Hendershott**, the dapper, musta-chioed Uncle Cranny, was the pianist and organist who provided musical interludes on shows including *Tune Time* on WEWS for 22 years starting in 1948. He played the organ and Gil Chase played the piano on the dinnertime *Twenty Fingers* series in the 1950s.

104. A Genie garage door opener or a snow blower were typical grand prizes on **"The Gene Carroll Show."**

105. The call letters of **WUAB (Channel 43)** refer to its original owner, United Artists Broadcasting.

106. **Soul Patrol:** When crime hit Cleveland in the 1970s, Channel 8 movie and comedy host "Big Chuck" Schodowski stepped into a smoke-filled telephone booth as mild-mannered Ed Tarboosh, and emerged as the caped black super hero Soul Man, played by videographer Herb Thomas.

107. Hall of Fame sportscaster **Mel Allen**, best known as The Voice of the Yankees from too many World Series, replaced Herb Score as Harry Jones' partner in the Indians' TV booth for the 1967 season. Allen was succeeded by Dave Martin in 1968.

Herb Score and Harry Jones, 1966

108. **"Television Cities"** was sometimes used to describe cities, like Cleveland, that had stations on the air at the end of the 1940s and start of the 1950s.

109. **TV Boom:** Cleveland jumped quickly at the chance to become a "Television City." Only about 300 TV sets were operating in town when WEWS went on the air in December 1947. By October 1948—when WEWS carried its first network programs from CBS, televised three Indians-Braves World Series games, and got its first rival in WNBK—the city had an estimated 12,000–15,000 sets, more than the national average.

110. **Holiday Tradition:** Choirs, figure skaters, laser shows, and even a singing Santa Claus have entertained crowds at Cleveland's annual Christmas lighting ceremony on Public Square. Channel 3 has made the event a TV tradition since 1985 with its live *'Tis the Season* special, presented at dinnertime on the evening after Thanksgiving.

1964 Christmas promo at TV3 including Mike Douglas, Jay Lawrence, Jerry G, Bud Dancy, Jim Runyon, Dick Goddard, Linn Sheldon, Carl Stern, Clay Conroy

111. **"The Giant Tiger Amateur Hour"** was the original title of *The Gene Carroll Show* in 1948. Under both titles, Carroll made his entrance through parted curtains while a "production number" chorus line danced to the theme song "Hold That Tiger"—for the sponsoring Giant Tiger discount stores.

112. **"Eugenia,"** a book review program hosted by Eugenia Thornton, was one of the early local programs on Channel 25.

113. *Remember when* Cleveland's UHF stations started by bringing viewers previously unseen talk-show hosts such as Joe ("Go gargle with razor blades") Pyne, the bearded and cigar-smoking Alan Burke, and genial Woody Woodbury?

114. **Flying Host:** Don Cameron, the host of Channel 5's *It's Academic* from 1964-71, commuted to tapings from Toronto—since producers and sponsors wanted the host to have no association with other products or programs in Cleveland. He was succeeded by Don Webster, Steve Wolford, Lou Maglio and, for a second term, Webster.

115. **Jack Perkins** gained national notice as an NBC news correspondent and as the white-bearded, avuncular host of *Biography* on cable's A&E Network. Cleveland saw him first as the young and somewhat gangly former WGAR radio reporter who anchored the 11 p.m. news on Channel 5 in the late 1950s and early '60s with George Grant and professorial-looking John B. Hughes.

Channel 5 news trio, from top: Jack Perkins, George Grant, John B. Hughes

116. **TV's Radio Days:** WKYC (Channel 3) and WJW (Channel 8) used to be co-owned with radio stations with which they shared call letters, facilities, and some on-air personalities. Channel 3's sister stations were sold by NBC in the early 1970s; they are now WTAM (AM 1100) and WMJI (FM 105.7). Channel 8's radio sisters were sold a few years later by Storer Broadcasting; they are now WRMR (AM 850) and WQAL (FM 104.1).

117. **Chain of Ghouls:** Ghoulardi was the most famous, the Ghoul was the loudest, but the longest-running costumed horror-movie host in Northeast Ohio is the Son of Ghoul, Keven Scarpino. He was first seen on Channel 67 in Canton in 1987, then moved to the low-power "CAT" stations WAX (Channel 35) in Cleveland and WAOH (Channel 29) in Akron.

118. *Remember when* stations displayed a "Please Stand By" or "One Moment Please" card, played music and had an announcer say they were "experiencing technical difficulties" when something went wrong with the signal?

119. **"See and Hear"** was the radio and TV column by Stan Anderson, the first television critic in the *Cleveland Press*.

120. **Maestro Millbrook** was the cartoon spokesman for locally baked Millbrook bread in the early 1960s. Under a puffed fringe of white hair topped by a white baker's hat, the Maestro wore a high collar, frock coat, vest, and billowing tie. He promoted the fact that "miracle mix" Millbrook was "baked to music."

121. The call letters of **WQHS (Channel 61)** stand for Quality Home Shopping.

122. *Recollection: Soupy Sales.* Soupy Sales has the face that launched a thousand pies. The whole act started for him sometime around 1950, when he was working under the name Soupy Heinz as the morning host on WJW radio and learning the infant medium of TV on WXEL (Channel 9). The studio was in Parma then, he recalled, and "we would go outside and do all these live bits. One day this farmer next door said, 'Why don't you use my horse on your show?' I said, "Why don't you bring him around tomorrow?" The farmer did. Soupy, as "Son of Cochise," staged a *Broken Arrow* parody in which, dressed as a Native–American, he rode up to a soldier, dismounted, said "White man come to Indian country, you kill our reindeer and our antelope, what is left for the Indian?" and got a pie in the face. The pie, he noted, was made by cooking host Alice Westin. "In those days, they didn't have shaving cream aerosol, that didn't come in until 1954 or '55, so you had to use whipping cream or egg whites," Soupy said. "That's where I started with the pies, out at 'XEL in Parma. It was really wild."

123. **TV's fastest cancellation** was issued in February 1969 when *Turn-On*—an attempt by ABC to copy the success of *Rowan and Martin's Laugh-In*—was pink-slipped between its eastern and West Coast feeds. WEWS took much of the credit (or blame). Asserting that its switchboard was jammed by outraged viewers, general manager Don Perris fired off a telegram saying the show wouldn't appear again on his station. "If your naughty little boys have to write dirty words on the wall," he wrote, "please don't use our walls." Coincidentally, the show's first and only guest host was Cleveland's Tim Conway.

124. **Mister Nickelsworth** was Captain Penny's off-screen railroad side-kick. The show's directors—Earl Keyes and Jim Breslin—provided his voice. Kids were invited to send in their artistic conceptions of what he looked like.

125. **No Live Shot:** When a report from the 1985 National League playoffs showed Elizabeth Taylor in the crowd, a WEWS sportscaster quipped, "Where's Dick? He's nowhere to be seen." Richard Burton, Taylor's two-time ex-husband, was busy being dead—and had been for a year. Taylor had meantime married and divorced John Warner.

126. *Remember when* "film at 11" was what stations promised for their late newscasts, in the days before videotape displaced film and live shots began to displace much of the videotape?

127. *Signature Saying:* When an Indian homered and Jack Corrigan was calling the game on Channel 43, it was "Touch-'em-all time!"

128. *Remember when* the *Press* boasted in March 1981 that it was the first daily paper to carry listings for cable channels—though the listings appeared only in the Community Weekly section distributed to home-delivery subscribers?

129. **"Cleveland Vice,"** a spoof of NBC's hot series *Miami Vice*, came to *Saturday Night Live* in a skit courtesy of writer (and Lorain native) Don Novello. Better known as Father Guido Sarducci, Novello had detectives trying to catch a culprit stealing bowling balls from Buckeye Lanes. Instead of driving Ferraris, the cops rode the bus. A "guest star" in the skit was Joan Rivers—a stock impression by regular Terry Sweeney—who said, "It's so cold here, I have to take off my pantyhose with an ice pick."

130. **SuperHost's Start:** Original WUAB staff announcer Marty Sullivan created "SuperHost" while clowning around in the studio one day in 1969. In baggy red satin shorts and size 13 sneakers, the Superman knock-off hosted *The Three Stooges* and other Saturday afternoon features on Channel 43 in its "We Play Favorites" years. Sullivan, a Detroit native who moved to Cleveland as a WGAR radio announcer in 1963, retired in 1993.

131. **"The Clear Fountain,"** light, classical flute music, was the theme for *Barnaby, Popeye & Friends*.

132. **Bozo the Clown** was not one character but a nationwide franchise. In Cleveland, the character was played on Channel 8 in the 1950s and early '60s by Ed Fisher. He achieved wider fame on WJW radio as the bow-tied, piano-playing morning host who also called himself E. Floyd Fisher and was known for his daily "Grouch Club" segments of comedy records.

133. **The Bell Tolls:** Channel 25 always made sure to start and end its live programs before and after the hour—its first studios were in the Max S. Hayes Vocational School on Cleveland's West Side, and viewers would otherwise hear the bell and the sound of classes changing. Channel 25 signed on the air as the nation's 100th public TV station (and Cleveland's first ultra-high frequency station) on Feb. 7, 1965.

134. *And now, a word from our sponsor:* "See-e-e the USA . . . in a C. Millah Chevuhlet!" East Side Chevy dealer Charlie Miller squawked the lines in a bad impression of Dinah Shore; lest anyone miss the point, he extravagantly threw the audience a kiss in best Dinah fashion. But Miller, a bald Tennessee native with a hick persona, didn't stop there in distinctive commercials that started running on Channel 61 in 1969. Among his better-remembered stunts, he popped out of a cornfield like a character on *Hee-Haw*, stood bare-chested wearing a barrel, donned a private-eye trench coat and snap-brim hat, played Baby New Year, played Cupid, wore a cowboy hat and rode a horse, peered into a crystal ball like a fortune-teller, dressed like a firefighter, pretended to be president, and wore a Superman costume. The ads made Miller a local institution into the 1980s—and such an instant celebrity that TV-5's then-new *Morning Exchange* held a "Charlie Miller Film Festival" in 1972.

135. **Big Ralph:** After WKYC ("KY 11") disc jockey Jerry G left for Chicago, colleague Jay "Jaybird" Lawrence took over as host of Channel 3's *Jerry G & Co.* The name had to change, so Lawrence changed it to *The Big Ralph Show*—explaining that Big Ralph was the name of his horse.

136. **Hometown Flavor:** Northeast Ohioans enjoyed picking out references to familiar places and things when the 1990s brought, for the first time, three network series set in the area. ABC's post-World War II *Homefront* was set in River Run, based on producer Bernard Lechowick's hometown, Mentor. NBC's comedy *3rd Rock from the Sun* was set at a college inspired by Kent State University, the alma mater of series creator and Toledo native Bonnie Huff Turner, and ABC's *Drew Carey Show* is set in Carey's native Old Brooklyn.

137. **Big-time Appetites:** Professional wrestlers taping shows at Channel 43 in the 1970s were not welcome everywhere when they went for post-bout meals at restaurants near the station on Day Drive in Parma. The jumbo grapplers were banned from the old Sweden House restaurant because it was an all-you-can-eat smorgasbord.

138. **The Glasses Cam** was the most memorable part of Channel 19's first newscast in February 1995. Reporter Dave Barker wore horn rims concealing a tiny camera to report on the lack of security at a local school that he entered without challenge.

139. **Cannonball:** It turned into a literal federal case when Channel 5 aired a 15-second clip of a local performance by Hugo "The Human Cannonball" Zacchini being shot out of a cannon in 1972. Though the station said "you really need to see (the act) in person to appreciate it," Zacchini sued Channel 5 for televising his act without permission. Five years later, the U.S. Supreme Court ruled on a 5–4 vote that stations could be sued for televising "a performer's entire act"—even a 15-second one. In 1979, the station settled with Zacchini for an undisclosed amount; he was seeking $275,000.

140. **Ben Crazy:** Even viewers who can't remember the medical drama *Ben Casey*, which ended its network run in 1966, know Channel 8's continuing comic skits featuring Big Chuck Schodowski as Dr. Ben Crazy. The skits always start with a parody of the original show's opening, which has Dr. Zorba solemnly intoning, "Man . . . woman . . . birth . . . death . . . infinity," while chalking appropriate symbols on a blackboard. Ben Crazy adds a dollar sign, followed by cackling laughter, and the sound of a cash register.

141. *And now, a word from our sponsor:* Or maybe not. Flamboyant auto dealer Rick Case made waves in November 1984 when he created an ad offering a free rifle or shotgun with the purchase of an all-terrain vehicle. Most local TV stations refused to carry it. "It's not like we're giving away Saturday night specials," a Case spokesman said. "These are not handguns. The ads are not designed to attract kids in here so we can give them a Winchester. The whole idea is to appeal to the outdoorsman, the hunter and the farmer . . . We anticipate a lot of the Winchesters will be given as nice Christmas gifts."

142. **"Knob location"** was the term in use for dial position on TV sets when Channel 3—then called WNBK—moved from Channel 4 in April 1954. The switch was made to avoid interference with Channel 5 in Cleveland and Channel 4 in Detroit after WNBK became the most powerful station in the Midwest, broadcasting with 100,000 watts from a 905-foot tower.

143. **STAR LOG, III.** Still more Northeast Ohioans who've made it big: TNN talker Ralph Emery, supermodel Angie Everhart, Cristina Ferrare (*Home and Family*), Joe Flynn (*McHale's Navy*), Miriam Flynn (*Maggie*), CNN correspondent Bob Franken, producer Woody Fraser (*Good Morning America*), Holly Fulger (*Anything But Love*), Teri Garr (*Good & Evil*), Bob Golic (*Saved by the Bell: The College Years*), Arsenio Hall (*Martial Law*), CNN anchor Leon Harris, Steve Harvey (*The Steve Harvey Show*), Patricia Heaton (*Everybody Loves Raymond*), John Henton (*The Hughleys*) . . .

144. Don't let anyone tell you they watched the entire **1948 World Series**, when the Indians beat the Boston Braves, on TV. Channel 5 telecast the games in Cleveland, but fans back home could not watch the games from Boston—ABC did not have a coaxial hookup between the two cities.

Fans watched the 1948 World Series through an audio feed and "re-creation" on this studio scoreboard at WEWS.

145. **Local viewers** received both a compliment and a snub upon learning that the long-running medical series *St. Elsewhere* was almost set in Cleveland instead of Boston. Dr. John Luria of the Cleveland Clinic was the show's medical advisor, and he let its creators, friends John Falsey and Joshua Brand, spend two weeks gathering background there. But Falsey went to college in Boston, and executive producer Bruce Paltrow said, "Boston has a little more snap. Lots of great hospitals in Cleveland, understand, but not the snap."

146. **The Trouble Is Not In Your Set**: Clevelanders missed the first network telecast of a World Series. It appeared on NBC in 1947—months before WEWS went on the air, and a year before NBC launched WNBK-TV in Cleveland.

147. *Remember when* TV hosts used to thank viewers for "inviting us into your living room"?

148. The game show **"Cash Explosion"** hit town like, yes, an explosion on Saturday nights on Channel 5 in the mid-1980s. It frequently ranked among the most-watched programs of the week—not because of the tuxe-doed hosts or bleachers filled with cheering friends of contestants, but because of its climax, the Ohio Lottery's Lotto drawing. The format of *Cash Explosion* kept changing to keep it interesting or at least watchable; as a lottery game, it can involve neither skill nor knowledge, only pure luck.

149. **Woodrow the Woodsman**, played by Clay Conroy, is instantly recognized by his luxuriant mustache and medieval-looking costume with tights and broadax—not to mention a distinctive wig that could have been borrowed from Prince Valiant and Moe Howard and lent to Pete Rose. Woodrow appeared daily from 1960 to 1966 on Channel 3, where he was hired as Barnaby's sidekick, and returned with new shows in a revival on Channel 8 in 1997.

150. *Recollection: Linn Sheldon,* on the early days of local TV: "We never thought of being personalities, celebrities. I was standing out front of WEWS, after we'd been on a few months, and a man and his wife and little child came by. He said, 'How about a picture?' I was so thrilled. Then he handed me the camera—they wanted me to take a picture of them with their camera."

151. **Duquesne beer**, based in Pittsburgh, sponsored Dorothy Fuldheim's nightly commentaries on WEWS. She sat at a desk bearing its logo and name, later shortened to Duke.

152. *Recollection: Big Wilson.* Actor Jack Riley, best known as deadpan neu-
rotic Elliot Carlin on *The Bob Newhart Show*, recalls starting in broadcasting
as a writer and producer for Big Wilson—the jumbo-sized cut-up on
Westinghouse's KYW radio and TV who was known as Jack to friends but
was actually named Malcolm. "When Westinghouse came into Cleveland,
geez, you never saw promotion like that. It seemed like every billboard, just
unbelievable. I don't know what the actual numbers were, but I think Biggie
had like over 60 percent of the morning radio audience. He was like God.
'Hey, you ARE big,' is what they always used to say. He was like Willard
Scott before Willard—he had that kind of thing going—and the station used
to use him anytime and anyplace they could. He was on the radio from 6 to
10 a.m. He'd go home and rest and come back for another show on TV
called *Six O'Clock Adventure*, with 'Sheena, Queen of the Jungle.' Then he'd
go home and come back at 11:20 at night for a 10-minute live show to fill
the time between the local news and Jack Paar, with his piano and sometimes his dog under the piano. We did anything we wanted. We'd do some

skits, god-awful skits, we'd provide our own props because there was nobody to help us, and then he had to be back the next morning at 5:30. Television was more fun to watch then—more human."

Linn Sheldon, Erica Toth of Ice Capades and Big Wilson, 1958.

153. Only about **300 TV sets**—most of them in bars and retail showrooms— were in Cleveland when its first station, WEWS (Channel 5), officially began operation on December 17, 1947. The first night's telecast included film from a Browns game and a travelogue. Then, said the announcer: "This is television station WEWS, your Scripps Howard station, first in Cleveland. WEWS operates on Channel 5 from 76 to 82 megacycles and maintains studios on East 13th street in downtown Cleveland. On this, the first telecast in Ohio, we take you to Public Hall, for the annual *Cleveland Press* Christmas party with Jimmy Stewart."

Jimmy Stewart, Jack Howard (president of Scripps Howard Radio) and general manager James Hanrahan.

154. **"It's Academic,"** launched in 1964, stakes a claim to being the longest-running local non-news show in Northeast Ohio. A weekend staple during the school year on Channel 5, the high-school quiz show changed its title to *Academic Challenge* for several years after Ohio Edison joined the Cleveland Electric Illuminating Company as a sponsor and the show's area for participating high schools widened.

155. *Remember when* stations signed off the air soon after midnight? The typical end-of-day ritual included a "sermonette" and playing of the National Anthem—followed by a test pattern and "snow."

156. **A 1977 hostage situation** in Warrensville Heights got nastier when Channel 8 aired a report showing police sharpshooters and cruisers outside the scene; negotiations for the release of the hostage stalled for a day when the hostage taker saw the telecast.

157. Nobody said **"DOR!othy"** like Ghoulardi, and nobody in Cleveland doubted for a moment that he was talking about Dorothy Fuldheim—the first local TV personality for whom one name said it all. Ironically, the real first name of her WEWS colleague Paige Palmer was also Dorothy—but Palmer chose to use Paige, her middle name, for TV.

158. **The Action-Cam,** a portable camera with accompanying van to transmit live TV pictures from a news scene, appeared in Cleveland in November 1973. Channel 5 was the first to have one; some of its early Action-Cam stories were New Year's Eve celebrations in Public Square, a Brecksville teachers' strike, and traffic jams. In 1979 Channel 5 added a new wrinkle to the Action-Cam—broadcasting from a helicopter.

159. **Home games of the Cleveland Indians** appeared on Channel 5 in 1949 thanks to sponsorship of Cleveland's Leisy Brewing Company.

160. **Reggie Rucker** went into sportscasting after ending his playing days with the Browns, but baseball fans were less than cheered when he tried his hand at Indians telecasts. "He was stultified," Rucker said, in a characteristic comment when an infielder lost sight of a fly ball.

161. **Gone, Not Forgotten:** Sports fans and most of Northeast Ohio mourned in August 1994 when sportscaster Nev Chandler lost a long battle with liver cancer at age 47. Chandler, remembered for both his professionalism and his sense of humor and mimicry, continued working on air through most of his illness. He joined WEWS in 1971 and became its sports director in 1985, served as radio voice of both the Indians and the Browns, and was named Ohio Sportscaster of the Year four times.

162. **STAR LOG, IV.** Good grief! More stars from Northeast Ohio: Hal Holbrook (*Evening Shade*), Bob "Mr. NBC" Hope, Billy Hufsey (*Fame*), A.J. Jamal (Comedy Central), Melina Kanakaredes (*Providence*), Carol Kane (*Taxi*), Dana King (*Day & Date*), Sarah Knowlton (*Working*), writer-producer Bernard Lechowick (*Homefront*), critic Stu Levin (*Entertainment Tonight*), Clea Lewis (*Ellen*), John Lithgow (*3rd Rock from the Sun*), NBC executive Rick Ludwin, ESPN football analyst Paul Maguire, writer-actor Pat McCormick (*The Tonight Show*) . . .

163. **Our Man Mark** replaced *3 on the Town* on Channel 3 in 1968 and featured Mark Russell, later known for his PBS comedy specials, as host, interviewer, and piano-playing entertainer.

164. *Remember when* if you missed a favorite show, you really missed it, because there were no VCRs?

165. *Recollection: Alan Freed.* Thirty years before Cleveland's Nina Blackwood became one of the original "veejays" on MTV in 1980, TV's first veejay was flopping—in Cleveland. Ironically, he was disc jockey Alan Freed, who later became legend by coining the term "rock and roll" for the rhythm and blues records on the "Moondog" show he launched on WJW radio in June 1951. Freed, who grew up in Salem, Ohio, had become a success as host of "Request Review" on Akron's WAKR-AM in 1945, and tried to jump to WADC-AM (now WTOU) in 1950. When a contract dispute kept him from working within 75 miles of Akron for a year, he landed a job at WXEL (Channel 9)—where he washed out as midday movie host, a notably inattentive announcer, and a "teejay" spinning popular records.

166. **"Moon Over Parma,"** the original theme to *The Drew Carey Show*, was written in 1973 for *The Hoolihan & Big Chuck Show* by Robert "Mad Dog" McGuire, a Cleveland jazz performer and music teacher. Carey first heard it performed by McGuire at the House of Swing ("Where Jazz Is King") in South Euclid.

167. **George E. Condon**, later a columnist and author, was the first TV critic for *The Plain Dealer*.

168. Channel 8 got calls complaining it wasn't paying its staff enough when weekend anchor **Eleanor Hayes** was seen moonlighting at a local McDonald's. She was actually training, at a family-owned franchise, to become a McDonald's owner-operator before leaving TV news in late 1993.

169. **Busted:** In 1977, WEWS sent out reporters Marge Banks and Tappy Phillips dressed as prostitutes to report on a police crackdown on streetwalkers. Ten minutes after hitting the street, they were arrested—for prostitution. Another Channel 5 reporter had to call police and explain the stunt to get the women released.

170. **"Monday Night Football"** upset Clevelanders in 1990 by running a halftime spot that had *Coach* star Jerry Van Dyke declaring, "I think the problem with Cleveland is, even if you win, you lose. You still got to go home to Cleveland." The Browns beat Denver, 30-29, and Mayor Michael White wrested an apology from ABC—Van Dyke went on the air two weeks later, before a Browns–Bengals game, to declare that he loved Cleveland. When asked who would win, he put a sack over his head and muttered, "The Browns don't have a shot." The Bengals won, 34–13.

171. *And now, a word from our sponsor:* "P.O.C., the . . . Pride of Cleveland!"
So went the commercial jingle for Cleveland's now-defunct Pilsener
Brewing Company, though not everyone agreed on exactly what P.O.C.
stood for. Some argued it meant "Pilsener Of Cleveland," but others
thought the letters stood for "Pride Of Cleveland" or "Pilsener On Call."

172. **NewsHawk 3** was Channel 3's helicopter in Cleveland TV's first "chopper
war," when the TV stations tried to outdo each other by leasing helicop-
ters. It tipped and crashed from low altitude during a snowstorm in
Ashtabula County in 1981, slightly injuring veteran reporter Joe Mosbrook
and videographer Dave Hollis.

173. **The Enchanted Forest**, with its wishing well and talking animals, was the home of Barnaby and Woodrow.

174. *Remember when* you improved TV reception by turning the rooftop antenna with a remote-control TenaRotor? And put strips of tape on the set-top circular dial to mark the best position for each station? And heard the rotor mechanism grind against caked-on ice in the winter?

175. **Jerry G & Company:** Students from a different high school each Saturday evening were the featured dancers on Channel 3's *Jerry G & Co.*, a half-hour music show inspired by the success of Channel 5's *Upbeat*. Students danced on low, circular white stages, each large enough to accommodate one couple.

176. **Emmett Miller,** one of the original anchors when WOIO started its own newscasts in February 1995, did not simply move to another station when he was dropped in favor of a two-woman team. He became host of the nationally syndicated *Strange Universe* program—which, ironically, was carried on WOIO—and also appeared as a news anchor in the feature film *Wag the Dog*.

177. **Jovi-Al:** Slimmer than he would become on NBC's *Today* show—but even then possessing a super-size personality and sense of humor that could turn the worst weather into a laughing matter—Al Roker made Cleveland his adopted hometown as the *Action 3 News* forecaster from 1979 to 1983.

Action 3 News, 1981: a thin Al Roker, Mona Scott, Dave Patterson, Doug Adair, Joe Pellegrino.

178. **Jenny Crimm** became Cleveland's first female street reporter and anchor on Channel 8 in the late 1960s. Tall, talented, and known for her antic and punning sense of humor, she moved on to Chicago and San Francisco before returning home in the mid–1970s and joining Channel 5, where she long anchored the noon news.

179. **Pete Carey**, a reporter and news director for radio stations WABQ and WJMO, became Cleveland's first black TV reporter when WJW hired him during the Hough riots in 1966. One of the first reporters to deliver a story live from the scene, Carey also served as assignment editor, producer, and public-affairs host before retiring in 1991.

180. Anchor **Bill Jacocks** always ended newscasts on Channel 5 by giving a vigorously confident "thumbs up" when the camera pulled back for a wide shot of the anchor team.

181. **"The Barn-Wood Playhouse"** teamed Barnaby and Woodrow for two hours on Saturday morning on TV-3 until 1965. More than an hour of each show was live with a studio audience, and the show was hugely popular with grown-ups as well as kids. Audiences awaited such live treats as seeing Barnaby—who usually played the ukelele—play the violin and use the bow to "accidentally" lift off Woodrow's wig.

182. **Rachel Van Cleve** sang opera arias while she cooked as a program hostess on Channel 5 in the 1950s.

183. Forecasting weather is notoriously dicey on the North Coast, and years of experience have made **Dick Goddard** the most popular and trusted meteorologist in Northeast Ohio. But Channel 8 hit a snag when it put tongue in cheek and erected "Believe in Goddard" billboards with a bold lightning bolt. Some viewers complained that the pun was sacreligious, and the campaign ended.

184. **Channel 61** rose from the ashes of darkened WKBF in 1981 as WCLQ, giving Cleveland its first taste of pay-per-view called "Preview." The station broadcast normally during the day, and at one point launched a big campaign for its *Dallas* reruns. At night, however, it scrambled its signal for "subscription television," and viewers who paid for decoders got to watch spicy movies into the wee hours. Not enough did: WCLQ was sold and evolved into home-shopping station WQHS.

185. **The Folkswagon** is the white van that carries Del Donahoo and crew around northeast Ohio for his "Del's Folks" and "Del's Feasts" reports on Channel 3. Such is his popularity that 116 cities and towns proclaimed his 65th birthday "Del Donahoo Day," on November 15, 1988, and that he was still with the station after 31 years in 1999, and signing a new, multi-year contract.

186. *Remember when* TV sets were furniture, designed to match the rest of a room's decor? And they had names, such as the Metropolitan, Envoy, Holiday, Cosmopolitan, International Modern, Wedgewood, Belvedere, Riviera, and Lido.

187. The call letters of **WEWS [Channel 5]** honor Edward Willis Scripps, founder of the company that has always owned the station, Scripps Howard.

WEWS logo, 1957

188. **P·A·R·RMA?!** In 1963, Ernie Anderson turned the name of the suburb where he once lived into a punch line on *Ghoulardi* after his buddy and collaborator Chuck Schodowski moved there. Fearing the wrath of neighbors when Anderson launched into a tirade about white socks and pink lawn flamingos, Schodowski cut off his microphone and played the polka "Who Stole the Kishka?"

189. **Wilbur Whiffenpoof** was the piano-playing railway station agent played by Earl Keyes, who served as a sidekick when Ron Penfound began hosting *Captain Penny's Fun House* on Channel 5 in December 1957.

Captain Penny with Earl Keyes as Wilbur Whiffenpoof

190. **Channel 5's first studios** were in the former Women's City Club on East 13th Street north of Euclid Avenue, marked by a vertical WEWS sign extending from the side of the building. The station moved in 1957 to a facility that was touted as the most modern "between New York and Chicago," at 3001 Euclid Avenue.

191. **Fred DeBrine** was the news anchor on Channel 5 after the departure of Bill Jorgensen and before the introduction of matinee idol John Hambrick with *Eyewitness News*.

192. **"The Old Redhead"** was Tom Manning. Best remembered for his Indians play-by-play on WTAM radio and his World Series broadcasts, he appeared as a sportscaster on the old WNBK-TV in the 1950s.

193. Thanks to **big oval letters reading KYW** and later WKYC, not to mention the "National Broadcasting Company" sign, Clevelanders think of the old East Ohio Gas Building at 1403 East 6th Street as the Channel 3 building. The station originally was located in the Superior Building, at East 9th Street and Superior Avenue, and plans to begin the 21st century in new quarters on Lakeside Avenue.

194. **"Arriving and Leaving,"** one of the first local programs on WEWS, featured station jack-of-all-trades Paul Hodges interviewing people who were—yes—arriving and leaving at the Greyhound bus station. Bums who felt their privacy was being violated by the TV camera migrated to the benches of the railway terminal at Terminal Tower.

195. *Remember when* your TV set was part of a "home entertainment center" that also included a radio and a hi-fi record player?

196. *Recollection: Linn Sheldon.* Linn Sheldon, a stage and film actor and cabaret performer, was an original on-air employee of WEWS. "We had no one to copy, and the ideas just flowed," he said. "We didn't worry about the news because the news was rip and read. We'd lip-synch records, we did game shows, we did plays live, right in the studio. In 1948, I was doing the (sign-on) opening and telling people what's coming up, and I did a lip-synch of Jimmy Durante. A guy walked in a couple of days later and said, 'Can you do that three times a week for 15 minutes?' His name was Fred Shaw, from Rogers jewelry stores, and that was the first sponsored show in Cleveland—I lip-synched records three times a week."

197. **The Haley Shuffle** was Tom Haley's soft-shoe daily dance of dawn on Channel 3's *Today in Cleveland*—usually a solo, but sometimes performed with a visitor or crew member.

198. *News Flash:* In 1958 on TV-3 news, Jim Graner substituted for Bob Neal as sportscaster, joining anchor Pete French and weatherman Joe Finan. Finan promised to rattle the famously unflappable Graner, and arranged for a woman in a raincoat to stand in front of him. Fifteen seconds into the sports cast, she opened the coat—it was all she wore. "I had the Indians playing the Browns," Graner quipped later.

199. **Animal House** was the signature flick of WOIO (Channel 19) when it went on the air in May 1985, promising movies "as only Nineteen can show them." That meant showing *Animal House* without any editing, a bold stroke that made a fast impression on local viewers.

200. **Still Running:** "King the Wonder Dog," the best known "Kielbasy Kid" skit from *The Hoolihan & Big Chuck Show*, features King racing through snow-bound woods to the rescue of Chuck's cowboy Kid, whose leg is trapped under a downed tree. The punch line: King doesn't even break stride upon reaching the Kid, but bounds over him and keeps going. The skit won Schodowski the first local Emmy, presented in 1969.

201. Country bandleader **Frank "Pee Wee" King** hosted *Ranch 10-0-2* on WEWS in the 1950s. Its name was derived from the sponsoring local beer, "Erin Brew Ten-Oh-Two," which was also a principal sponsor of Alan Freed's "Moondog" show on WJW radio. As the 90-minute *Pee Wee King Show*, it was fed from WEWS to ABC as a weekly Monday summer series in 1955, featuring King and His Golden West Cowboys, vocalist Redd Stewart, "shuffling cowboy" singer Neal Burris, and tall comedienne Little Eller. King's hits were "Tennessee Waltz" and "Slow Poke."

202. **Texas Jim** was the old cowboy character played by
WEWS producer-director Jim Breslin as a kiddie host
starting in the 1950s. He served as occasional sidekick
and fill-in for Captain Penny.

Courtesy of Channel 5

203. **Indians baseball** officially became more important
than world events such as trouble in Bosnia, federal
budget concerns, and the O.J. Simpson trial, in
October 1995, when Channel 3 preempted *NBC Nightly News* to run a
Tribe special.

204. **Freddy The Alli-Croc** was the alligator-crocodile named Frederick
Maximillion Gesundheit, one of Woodrow the Woodsman's puppet
pals in the Enchanted Forest. Among the others were Voracious, the
peanut-butter-and-jelly sandwich-eating elephant, and Tarkington
Whom II, the wise old owl.

205. **Striking Image:** Death notices, scrolling slowly up the screen during extended-length newscasts, were one of the ways stations tried to fill the void when a 129-day strike and shutdown kept the *Cleveland Press* and *The Plain Dealer* from publishing in the winter of 1962–1963.

206. **STAR LOG, V.** Next time some outlanders crack wise about Northeast Ohio, remind them of: Gates McFadden (*Star Trek: The Next Generation*), Marian Mercer (*It's a Living*), Burgess Meredith (*The Twilight Zone*), CBS consumer correspondent Erin Moriarty, Martin Mull (*Roseanne*), Paul Newman (*Goodyear Playhouse*), Don Novello (Father Guido Sarducci), CNN correspondent Eileen O'Connor, NBC correspondent Kelly O'Donnell, writers—and brothers—Steve O'Donnell (*Seinfeld*) and Mark O'Donnell (*Saturday Night Live*), Ed O'Neill (*Married With Children*), Jack Paar (*The Tonight Show*), Jack Perkins (*Biography*), Luke Perry (*Beverly Hills, 90210*), Norma Quarles (CNN, NBC), Jack Riley (*Rugrats*) . . .

207. *Remember when* only 40 Indians games were televised per season, through the 1970s on Channel 8?

208. **Joey Bishop** sat atop the TV world in the 1960s as star of a sitcom (*The Joey Bishop Show*), host of his own ABC talk show, and permanent guest host for Jack Paar and Johnny Carson. But the Bronx-born comedian got his start in Cleveland, at a suitable venue for a future Rat Pack mainstay—a club called El Dumpo, at 2119 Prospect Avenue.

209. The exterior shot of the **Winfred Louder** department store on *The Drew Carey Show* is actually the Halle building, site of the former department store on Playhouse Square. It was added in the show's second season.

210. **The DuMont Network** provided a
Metropolitan Opera telecast—the first
program seen when WXEL (Channel 9),
the precursor of WJW (Channel 8),
went on the air in 1949. DuMont went
out of business in 1954, mostly a vic-
tim of poor nationwide distribution. It
was best known for its wrestling
shows, *The Jackie Gleason Show* and
Bishop Fulton J. Sheen's program.

GRAY DRUG
NEWS PARADE

*Jimmy Dudley and Bob Long anchored
the "Gray Drug News Parade" at 7 p.m.
weeknights on WXEL in the early 1950s.*

211. Valentine's Day brought real-life wed-
dings annually to **"The Morning Exchange."**
Contest-winning couples exchanged vows on the show while invited
guests mingled with TV guests, who were as varied as Bob Feller and Rita
Moreno.

212. **Action Guy:** Tim Taylor had a different image before he became Channel 8's main anchor and after he was an Action Central News reporter on WHK radio. In the mid-1970s, he was Channel 5's "Action Reporter"—highlighting the station's new *Action-Cam* by reporting live from news scenes, donning an Afro-style hairdo and colorfully wide-striped shirtsleeves.

213. **Loose Lips:** "Ted is probably the nicest human being you can meet," Carole Meekins, a mischievous and popular WEWS news anchor, said of on-air partner Ted Henry in a *Plain Dealer* interview. "He's not phony and full of himself. Of course, it helps that we've slept together. You know," she added after a pause, "I'd better watch that. One of these days somebody's going to take me seriously." However they took her, station management did not appreciate the joke; she soon left for Milwaukee.

214. **Woozy Anchor:** WEWS helped the *Cleveland Press* beat *The Plain Dealer* to its own story in August 1965. News anchor Bill Jorgensen and cameraman Walt Glendenning chartered a boat to score an exclusive interview at sea with Robert Manry, a *PD* copy editor from Willowick who made worldwide headlines crossing the Atlantic alone in the 13-foot sailboat Tinkerbelle. The seasick Jorgensen's story ran on Channel 5 and on page one of the *Press*.

215. **"Judd's"** was the short-lived restaurant specializing in ribs that was opened by newscaster Judd Hambrick after the Texas native started his first stint in Cleveland in 1977. "I still cook them," he said after the eatery closed. "I just don't sell them commercially anymore."

216. *Remember when* Channel 3 news anchor Virgil Dominic delivered the national network news from Cleveland every weekday at 3 p.m. on NBC radio?

217. **"The Mike Douglas Show"** went on the air on TV-3 in January 1961 as a slicker, more showbiz-oriented challenge to Channel 5's *1 O'Clock Club*. Boasting a different big-name guest co-host every week, the show became a hit locally and then in national syndication. Production moved to Philadelphia with Westinghouse in 1965, and the show began moving TV-3's schedule out of its familiar early after-noon slot.

218. *Remember when* you'd repair your TV by opening up the back and testing its vacuum tubes in a machine at the local drugstore?

219. **Soap Opera:** Liz Richards couldn't hide the trouble in her marriage to radio shock jock Gary Dee the day she showed up with a black eye on *The Morning Exchange*. On-air partner Fred Griffith was going through a divorce about the same time, and Joel Rose's problems also wound up on the air. "We were like *Peyton Place* there for a while," Fred said.

220. *Recollection: Chuck Schodowski.* As co-host of WJW's (Channel 8) *Big Chuck & Lil' John Show* since 1979, John Rinaldi has been half of Cleveland's most enduring on-air partnership—not to mention a valued station representative and local celebrity always ready to lend his time and energy to good causes. But his real job, all along, has been running Rinaldi Jewelers on E. 9th Street. He got the TV gig after appearing on skits on *The Hoolihan & Big Chuck Show.* Chuck Schodowski recalled how they first got together: "I wanted to do a skit based on this song 'Bridget the Midget.' And so I called a dance instructor and asked him if he had some female midgets. He said, 'No, but I got this short guy.' So he sent him over and the guy did the skit wearing a blond wig."

221. **"Biggie"** was a nickname on a nickname for KYW's "Big" Wilson. To viewers in the late 1950s, it also was the big sandwich advertised by the El Dorado drive-in on Northfield Road.

222. **Radical Jerry Rubin**, the "Yippie" leader of the 1960s was condescending, baiting, and then astonished when Dorothy Fuldheim bounced him from an interview for referring to police as "pigs." Climaxing with an angry Fuldheim pointing to the door, the incident was replayed often by Channel 5 over the years, but no one saw the aftermath—since the cameraman diligently stopped rolling when Fuldheim said, "stop the interview."

223. *Remember when* news anchors would sometimes smoke on camera?

224. **Battling Bills** were Cleveland's competing TV critics in the late '60s through the 1970s. Bill Barrett, caricatured in a bow tie at the top of his column, covered the tube for the *Cleveland Press*. Bill Hickey was the exacting TV wordsmith in *The Plain Dealer*. Ray Hart in the *PD* and Harriet Peters in the *Press* backed them up with reporting on the local scene.

225. The Baby Doctor, **Dr. Benjamin Spock**, was on the faculty of the Western Reserve University College of Medicine when he dispensed child-care advice on *Dr. Spock*, a Sunday afternoon show telecast to the nation on NBC from Cleveland's KYW. The show ran from October 1955 to August 1956.

226. **Hank the Rooster** crowed his morning wake-up for viewers of WKYC's *Today in Cleveland*, with Del Donahoo and Tom Haley, until the show ended in 1997. He got his name from popular Henry "Hank" Zbrzeski, a longtime sound technician at the station.

227. *Recollection: Dick Clark.* Dick Clark was a disc jockey on WFIL-AM in Philadelphia when he stepped in as substitute host of TV's *Bandstand* for the first time in late 1955. He became permanent host in July 1956, a few months after the regular host was arrested for driving while intoxicated. "The wonderful irony for Cleveland is that I had just applied to WEWS, telling (the late general manager) Jim Hanrahan that I was the guy who

does the radio version of the *Bandstand* show that's so successful, and I'd love to do a version in Cleveland," Clark said. "I just wanted to rip it off and go to Cleveland because I knew it would be a hit. He said, 'Are you kidding?' Turned me down flat. He literally threw me out of his office over the phone. He wasn't abusive, but he was so abrupt. It was the nicest thing anyone ever did for me, because I never would have gotten the other job. I'm indebted to him in a strange way. If he hadn't turned me down, the course of events might not have happened."

228. **"Today in Cleveland"** entertained early-rising viewers on Channel 3 for 18 years until its cancellation on Friday the 13th in June 1997. Hosts Tom Haley and Del Donahoo danced, wore funny hats, ate pastry and sent greetings to far-flung viewers, while still delivering news updates on the distinctively folksy broadcast.

229. **Harvey Pekar,** Cleveland comic book author (*American Splendor*) and social commentator, was almost a regular on David Letterman's NBC show in the mid-1980s. But he disappeared, in what NBC called "a little tiff," after baiting Letterman about the misdeeds of NBC owner, General Electric. When he returned as Cleveland's "always surly" and "always lovable" favorite son in April 1993, Dave asked how things were in Cleveland. "That's a real $15 million question, Dave," Harvey said. "What aspect of Cleveland life are you particularly interested in? You used to be a meteor-ologist in Indiana—would you be interested in the climate? The unemploy-ment situation, perhaps? The economy?" Said Letterman: "The air is crackling with good conversation tonight."

230. **King of Trivia:** The late Frank Dillon, a teacher for 34 years at South High School and a contributor of trivia features to *The Plain Dealer*, became TV's Game Show King from 195 appearances on various programs. A multiple national champion on *Joker's Wild* and *Jeopardy*, he always gave his winnings to charity. His final appearance, in 1993, made him the top winner on Bill Cosby's *You Bet Your Life*. "This ends my television career," Dillon said. "Time to leave well enough alone. But I wanted to go out on a winning note."

231. **His Town:** After musician Michael Stanley broke up his band in 1987, he became a correspondent on Channel 8's *PM Magazine* and co-host with Jan Jones of its short-lived successor, *Cleveland Tonight*.

232. **"Philco Television Playhouse,"** an NBC anthology series, greeted viewers who were watching on October 31, 1948, when WNBK (Channel 4), precursor of WKYC (Channel 3), went on the air.

233. **The father of Cleveland TV** was not Bill Wiedenmann. But you could get an argument on that at WEWS, where he was known to everyone as "Dad" or "Pop." Amiably cantankerous and universally admired, he spent more than 50 years at Channel 5 as a cameraman and director of news and local programs (starting in 1947), and trained generations of broadcasters. The station's new newsroom is dedicated to him.

234. The movie **"Field of Dreams"** inspired a slick and memorable *Big Chuck & Lil' John* parody. Chuck, playing a mustachioed old-time ballplayer, materializes from a cornfield and reacts in delight when he sees what John has been building in answer to a voice saying, "If you build it, he will come." As the skit closes, "it" turns out to be an outhouse from which Chuck emerges in smiling relief.

235. **"There he is!"** was the cry of the Giant Tiger dancers when Gene Carroll came through the curtains on his weekly amateur hour.

236. **Red Barber and Van Patrick** were the TV announcing team for 1948 Indians–Braves World Series. Sponsored by Gillette, the telecasts were available to "all stations" through cooperation of DuMont Television, NBC, CBS, ABC, and radio's Mutual Broadcasting System—though Cleveland had only one station, WEWS.

237. **Hugh Danaceau**, more recently news director of fine arts station WCLV-FM, quickly became the city's top TV political reporter after joining KYW in 1959. He served as host and commentator for Channel 25's live telecasts of Cleveland City Council meetings from 1968-77, then became host of *The Danaceau Report*, which evolved into *North Coast Report* on Channel 25. He also was the first regional correspondent for public TV's *Nightly Business Report*, helped launched an all-news format on WERE-AM, and was associated with Channel 5 and radio stations WJW and WWWE.

238. **The "Mile of Money"** was a Sohio contest of the 1960s whose frequently mentioned prize of $5,280 was the way a lot of kids came to know and remember how many feet are in a mile.

239. **"Who's the funny man?"** It was Cliff Norton—whose short *Funny Manns* films ran on Captain Penny's Fun House in the mid-1960s. The segment's opening showed Norton in a variety of guises and asked, "Which . . . one . . . will . . . he . . . be?"

240. **Newsroom 25** was Channel 25's only entry into the nightly news arena. Begun on January 2, 1975, it lasted several weeks, for the duration of the newspaper strike that inspired it. It featured Herb Kamm, Seymour Raiz, and Chuck Stella from the *Cleveland Press*, who read their stories on the air.

241. *And now, a word from our sponsor:* "Mah name . . . is Jewett Parmeter. Ah just won . . . ninety-eight thousan' . . . three-hunnert and FIFty dollars. All I done . . . was check the winner's list." Drawled in a somewhat nasal, Appalachian accent that rendered "list" as "lee-ust," this was the on-camera declaration by Parmeter after he won the Sohio "Winners List" jackpot in 1970. Endlessly repeated, the commercial made the aging Parmeter an improbable Ohio cult celebrity, famous for being famous.

242. **A favorite blooper** at WEWS came when news anchor Tom Field introduced a utility company commercial showing the "all-gas house of savings." The miscued film showed either a house on fire or logs burning—depending on who recalls the blooper, which wasn't recorded. What everyone remembers is that the giggling Field never regained his composure during the newscast.

243. **Timing Was Everything:** Channel 43 went on the air in 1968 from the old Parmatown Lanes, with its studio in a trailer parked outside. The announcing booth was inside the bowling alley, next to a men's room. A sign in the restroom said, "Don't flush while the announcer is on the air."

244. **"Bill Finn's Round the World Adventure"** series appeared on Channel 5 during late-evening hours in the mid-1950s, taking viewers to exotic locales before *Adventure Road* started on Channel 8.

245. **Cleveland City Council meetings** were a regular feature on Channel 25 through the 1970s—until speeches played for the camera resulted in marathon sessions and viewers started to lose interest.

246. *Remember when* UHF channels didn't click on the dial, but had to be zeroed in like radio stations?

247. **"Polka Varieties,"** hosted by Paul Wilcox and briefly by Tom Fletcher, replaced *The Frankie Yankovic Show* on Channel 5 starting in 1957. Running in the early 1980s and syndicated to 13 cities, the 60-minute Sunday show, featuring local bands and performers from around the world, was noted for audience members trying to dance into good camera position.

248. **String·a·ling:** Kids who visited Mr. Jingeling on Halle's seventh floor —and later at Higbee's and on The Avenue at Tower City Center— were given oversized cardboard keys with a red string attached.

249. **Digital broadcasting,** which has been mandated by the Federal Communications Commission to replace "analog" TV in 2006 after a seven-year conversion period, got a mixed reception when it arrived in Cleveland in June 1999. The first digital station, WKYC-DT, interfered with outdated cable converters and knocked out service to some 15,000 premium-cable subscribers in southwest suburbs.

250. The biggest shake-up in **Cleveland TV history** started on May 23, 1994, when New World Communications, then owner of WJW, announced a sweeping deal that would end the station's 38-year affiliation with CBS and align it with Fox Broadcasting—the station's eventual owner. The deal became reality at 5 a.m. on September 3, 1994, when WJW became a Fox affiliate, CBS moved to nine-year-old WOIO (Channel 19), and the Fox Kids Network shifted to WBNX (Channel 55).

251. **"TV Week"** was distributed on Fridays with *The Plain Dealer* while the *Press* was still in business. In the early 1960s, the listings magazine was one-fourth the size of a standard newspaper page, but was stapled "sideways" on its shorter edge as a top-of-set convenience.

252. **"TV Showtime"** was the *Reader's Digest*–sized listings guide with a glossy color cover that was distributed as a bonus on Fridays with the *Cleveland Press*. *Showtime* was also the name of the tabloid entertainment section in the Friday *Press*.

253. **Who killed Laura Palmer?** The answer to the mystery that caught up viewers when *Twin Peaks* became a sensation ended up being her nutty father, played by Akron native Ray Wise.

254. *And now, a word from our sponsor:* "The oranges ripen in the Florida sun, fresh on the tree they stay. And they pick 'em and they squeeze, just as fast as you please, and the Big O leaves the same day. Roll on, Big O—get that juice up to Lawson's in 40 hours. Roll on, Big O—get that juice up to Lawson's in 40 hours. One man sleeps while the other man drives, on the non-stop Lawson run. And the cold, cold juice in the tank truck caboose stays as fresh as the Florida sun. Roll on, Big O—get that juice up to Lawson's in 40 hours. Roll on, Big O—get that juice up to Lawson's in 40 hours." Who could drink frozen juice after hearing the most compelling—and certainly the most driving—local commercial jingle of the 1960s? It advertised the fresh bottled juice sold at Lawson's, the local convenience store chain that was sold to Dairy Mart in 1985. The commercial's scenes of Florida groves are less remembered than the sight of a gleaming tanker truck barreling down the highway—with a smiling driver bedding down behind the man at the wheel."

255. **Patty Rowe** was the local actress remembered by TV viewers as Soupy Sales' sidekick and for her local eyeglass commercials.

256. **Cleveland Indians telecasts** drew meager audiences through the 1980s but soared to the highest local ratings in Major League Baseball when dank Municipal Stadium gave way to packed Jacobs Field, and the team became must-see winners. The fourth game of the 1995 World Series, in which Atlanta beat the Tribe, 5-2, in Cleveland, became the most-watched baseball game in Cleveland history, seen in 61.8 percent of Northeast Ohio homes.

257. **"The Morning Bandwagon"** was the WTAM radio show featuring the station's staff orchestra, conducted by Henry Gordon, that was telecast on sister station WNBK-TV in the years before *Today* in the late 1940s and early '50s. Staff announcer Jay Miltner often lent his vibrant baritone as vocalist.

258. **Bob Franken,** an esteemed congressional reporter for CNN in the
'90s, was famous in 1978 for quitting Channel 8. Citing unnamed sources,
he had reported that National City Bank chairman Claude Blair was refus-
ing to help Cleveland in its financial crisis because Blair did not like Mayor
Dennis Kucinich. An unidentified bank official complained to Channel 8,
which broadcast a retraction and apology. Franken, standing by his story,
left the station.

259. **Sports anchor:** Dignified, low-key, and unflappable, silver-haired Jim
Graner was the thinking fan's sportscaster and a figure of stability on TV-3
starting in the late 1950s. Colleagues and viewers grieved when he faltered
from effects of a brain tumor that would claim his life in 1976, and
Channel 3 faltered with him. Its sports slot became a musical chair for
more than a decade, filled by John Henk, Joe Pellegrino, Tom Ryther, Paul
Rutigliano, Jim Mueller, and Wayland Boot, among others, until Jim
Donovan settled in for a long run.

260. **"Hello, Hello, Hello"** was the signature song that opened the "Gene &
Glenn" radio show of Gene Carroll and Glenn Rowell on WTAM in the
early 1930s. The music greeted a generation of youngsters whose
own children watched Carroll entertain as "Uncle Jake," in a diminu-
tive porkpie hat, on Channel 5 in the 1950s.

261. **Johnny Powers** became Cleveland's icon of professional wrestling in
shows broadcast on Channel 43 and hosted by Jack Reynolds until
1976. Pedro Martinez was the promoter and his son, Ronnie, was the
ring announcer for matches that featured the likes of villain Waldo
Von Erich. Good-guy Powers later returned to his native Canada and
became a stockbroker.

262. *Signature Saying:* On her commercial endorsements, Paige Palmer
said, "I want you, my customer, to have the best, so that you can be
forever young and beautiful."

263. **Akron's commercial TV station,** until 1988, had call letters tying it to its home city. Born as WAKR (Channel 49) in 1953 and later renamed WAKC after it moved to Channel 23, the station became WVPX by order of new owner Paxson Communications. Paxson wanted all its station names to include a "PX," tying them to its PAX-TV network.

264. **STAR LOG. VI.** Had enough of our ties to the TV Nation? Well, don't forget: Bumper Robinson (*Grown Ups*), Alan Ruck (*Spin City*), programming executive Lucie Salhany (Fox, UPN), CNN correspondent Martin Savidge, Golf Channel commentator Denny Schreiner, Molly Shannon (*Saturday Night Live*), ESPN anchor Bob Stevens, actor-director Betty Thomas (*Hill Street Blues*), writer-producer Bonnie Turner (*That '70s Show*), writer-producer Steve Wasserman (*Beverly Hills, 90210*), Jesse White (the Maytag repairman), Kym Whitley (*Sparks*), Fred Willard (*Fernwood 2-Night*), Ray Wise (*Twin Peaks*) and Barrie Youngfellow (*It's a Living*).

265. **"The following program** is brought to you in living color on NBC." So went the announcement in the early 1960s, when color shows were still designated by stars and boldface letters in TV listings. NBC became the first full-color network, so Channel 3 had the most color shows, but Cleveland's first local broadcasts in color appeared on Channel 8 in 1964.

Election night 1960 at Channel 8: Doug Adair and John Fitzgerald

266. **Newman's Own:** WJW started a five-minute news program called *Today's Top Story* to follow its late-evening *Sohio Reporter* in 1954. To do commercials for it, they hired a young blond actor from the Cleveland Play House to make his screen debut—Paul Newman.

267. **Tre Potsie** is Italian for Three Stooges. And that's how Captain Penny often referred to them, in grand fashion, while introducing their slapstick films. "We laugh at them—but we don't imitate them," he would caution.

268. **"Mushmouth" Mariano Pacetti** set the world's record for pizza eating—a 12-inch pie in 27 seconds—on *The Big Chuck & Lil' John Show*. Mush was previously beaten only twice by human challengers in the show's weekly competition, and both times reclaimed his title the following week. The only challenger he could not top was Chris, the Fairview Fireball—a German shepherd.

269. **"Now Hitting for Cleveland ...":** Ron Penfound, the announcer, weatherman and would-be sportscaster who was best known as Channel 5's Captain Penny, was heard but not seen as the Indians' announcer at Cleveland Stadium.

270. **"The Adventures of Johnny McQueen"** was Cleveland's own private-eye series, a weekly whodunit that ran for three months and won a big following on Sunday nights in the spring of 1957. Karl Mackey, later managing director of Lakewood Little Theater, starred as John Alexander McQueen. Noted for pre-taped "integrated commercials" in which Johnny praised whichever car he was driving between live interior scenes, the show was canceled during summer hiatus when sponsors—Chrysler-Plymouth-Dodge-DeSoto dealers—switched to *Highway Patrol*.

271. **"Distaff,"** defined as "a woman's work or domain," was Cleveland's first "woman's show." Hosted by Alice Weston and directed by Betty Cope, it debuted on Valentine's Day 1948 on WEWS. Years later, Weston recalled an episode where she tried to disguise that she had cut her hand during a cooking segment—and then heard her assistant, Ophelia Dudley Steed, praying on camera, "Dear God, please stop Miss Alice's hand from bleeding."

Ophelia Dudley Steed, Alice Weston's assistant, with Jim Kirkey, 1949.

272. **Jakies** was the derisive term used since the 1950s by Cleveland news photographers for the kids and bystanders who waved and crowded into shots on the street and in public places. It took on added meaning in 1994 when Jacobs Field opened and was dubbed "the Jake." Fans in field-level loges behind home plate waved for cameras on nearly every pitch.

273. **The Mary Hartman War:** *Mary Hartman, Mary Hartman*, a syndicated soap-opera parody from producer Norman Lear, met frequent controversy during its short run in the late '70s. Its comic subjects included a mass murder, a flasher, impotence, and a nervous breakdown by Mary herself (played by Louise Lasser). Controversy raged loudest in Cleveland when Channel 8 general manager William Flynn decided to air the show week nights at 7:30 in February 1977. Viewers protested, a priest called for a boycott of the station until it moved the show out of early evening, and newspaper columnists took up sides. A *Plain Dealer* TV critic called the show "the most stultifying piece of programming packaging ever to darken a cathode ray tube." Don Robertson of the *Press* argued, "There is still such a thing as the First Amendment, and if television can carry the obscenities of Vietnam and Watergate, it also can carry the absurdist nonsense of MH, MH." Flynn moved the show back to late-night hours after just a month, asserting that the program was doomed and that he had misjudged the audience: "Clevelanders are far more outgoing and friendly when you meet them than easterners," he said. "Yet collectively

they are far less tolerant of hearing the other person's point of view and certainly less open-minded when it comes to television programs."

274. **"Hickory Hideout"** was the award-winning local half-hour-long weekly show that greeted preschoolers on Channel 3 from 1982-90. The "hideout" was a treehouse where squirrel puppets Nutso and Shirley joined neighbors Know-It-Owl, human pals Cassandra Wolfe and Wayne Turney, and villain Buzz Buzzsaw for jokes, story-telling, original songs, and information.

275. Weather forecasters **Frank Cariello** of WUAB and **Don Webster** of WEWS revived an almost-forgotten local program idea when they started weekly broadcasts from backyard barbecues in 1989. In the early 1950s, WEWS aired *The Norge Block Party*, hosted by Bob Dale, featuring the Johnny Pecon Band playing polkas and standards in a different neighborhood every week.

276. **Making a Difference**: Viewers in the mid-1970s complained that they couldn't remember who was who when watching Channel 8's anchor team of Jeff Maynor and Jim Hale. Both were young and sported the era's puffed-out helmet-head hairdos. Hale grew a moustache to set himself apart.

277. **Time Was Short**: Channel 8 hoped to duplicate the success of TV-3's *Mike Douglas Show* with *Dale Young Time*, a morning variety show. Young, a singer from Detroit, hosted a studio audience in the Copa Theater-Restaurant near WJW on Playhouse Square. It lasted for one season.

Dale Young and Bwana Don Hunt

278. **A simple line drawing of a house** incorporating the letters "NET" often appeared on screen in the early days of Channel 25, signifying it was a member of National Educational Television, the predecessor of the Public Broadcasting Service.

279. Witty, opinionated and irrepressible, burly, bearded and brushcut, the gimlet-eyed **Don Robertson** brought provocative commentary, interviews, and movie and stage reviews to channels 3, 8, 25 and 61 through the 1960s and '70s. A reporter and columnist for *The Plain Dealer, Cleveland News* and *Cleveland Press*, he also wrote scripts for the soap opera *The Edge of Night* and was a prolific author. In the introduction to Robertson's novel *The Ideal Genuine Man,* Stephen King called called him one of his three greatest influences and one of America's best unknown published novelists. Of Robertson's 19 novels—now out of print, but available from libraries and book dealers—colleague Dick Feagler especially recommends *The Greatest Thing Since Sliced Bread* and *Praise the Human Season*. Robertson died after a long illness on his 70th birthday in March 1999.

280. **Bob Crumpler** was the Cleveland teacher who became a local Mr. Wizard as the host of the *Search for Science* series on WVIZ. He went on to host *NewsDepth*, WVIZ's weekly news series for middle school students, hosted a talk show on the old Channel 61, and became the first African-American reporter on WEWS. He left town to become a McDonald's franchiser in Detroit.

Courtesy of Channel 5

281. *And now, some words from our sponsors:*

"For jump and zoom in every step, get Keds, kids, Keds!"

"You can tell it's Mattel—it's swell!"

"GI Joe, GI Joe, fighting man from head to toe—on the land, on the sea, in the air."

"Deluxe Man-In-Space—complete with missile base! With astronauts and satellite, you send them into flight."

"Soaky soaks you clean, in oceans full of fun. Scubble-y, bubble-y, flibbity, flubble-ty, clean before you're done. Soaky soaks you clean, and every girl and boy gets a toy when it's empty! When it's empty, it's a toy."

"Ninety-nine squeezes, ninety-nine—makes the Brillo soap pad shine shine shine!"

"What walks down stairs/Alone or in pairs/And makes a slinky sound?/A spring! A spring! A marvelous thing!/Everyone knows it's Slinky./It gives a big lift/When wrapped as a gift,/A very likeable toy./Its falling in place brings smiles to your face./Something kids can enjoy."

"She drinks and wets and cries and frets!"

"Chocks, chum, is the vitamin—fruit flavored, take just one!"

"B-O! N-O! M-O! Oh oh oh! It's Bonomo—candy!"

"White Dove—it never needs turning!"

"When the value goes up up up! And the prices go down down down! Robert Hall this season, will show you the reason—high quality! Economy!"

"Sta-a-a-r Muffler! We want you to be quiet—quiet in your car! You're not far from a Star—no matter where you are!"

"You get a square deal, on every square yard, at Carpet Barn and Tile House!"

"I've got a Ford on my mind, mind, mind. Ed Mullinax is a friend of mine."

"Here he comes, here he comes, greatest toy you've ever seen! And his name is—Mister Machine!"

282. Channel 5's popular **Bob Dale** wore a whiskbroom-sized mustache to play kids' host Tim Twitter, a somewhat befuddled Civil War veteran, in the early 1950s.

283. *And now, a word from our sponsor:* "Mr. Jingeling/How you ting-a-ling/Keeper of the keys/On Halle's Seventh Floor/We'll be looking for/You to turn the keys." The ditty practically became a Christmas carol for kids in Cleveland, testimony to its effectiveness as a commercial for Halle's department stores. Mr. Jingeling—invented by a local ad agency in the mid-1950s—was a jolly, balding fellow who was supposed to keep the keys to Santa's workshop at the North Pole (as well as to the seventh floor toy department at Halle's). His five-minute show of puppets, songs and stories ran at dinner time in the weeks before Christmas on WEWS. The character actually outlived the Halle stores; played for eight years by Cleveland Play House actor and director Max Ellis, who died in the summer of 1964, Mr. Jingeling was taken over by the aptly named Earl W. Keyes, a producer-director at WEWS.

"Play Lady" Pat Dopp, Max Ellis, and Joe Berg on Mr. Jingleling set, 1960

284. **"Montage"** was the weekly feature documentary show that ran for 13 years on Channel 3, beginning in the late 1960s. One of Cleveland TV's most honored programs, it also was one of the highest-rated shows of its kind in the country.

285. **"AM Cleveland"** appeared at 9 a.m. weekdays on Channel 3 for seven years in the '80s and gave archrival *Morning Exchange* a run for its money. Hosted by Scott Newell and taped before a studio audience, the hour-long show featured contributions from soap-opera expert Lynda Hirsch, mixed with serious interviews and lighter features.

286. You never told mom you wanted **Bosco**, if you listened to Captain Penny. You were only to "suggest" that she purchase the chocolate syrup that sponsored his show.

287. Art anticipated life in 1978, when the *National Lampoon* published a Sunday newspaper parody for fictional **Dacron, Ohio**, that included a description of newscasts on local TV station WOIO—seven years before the real WOIO started. The fictional WOIO's "You Are Here" News was "shot with hand-held Mini-Cams . . . to create a looser, more immediate feel," on "a smart, futuristic set dominated by a backlit picture of computers, lights, monitors, oscilloscopes and the Cleveland skyline"—remarkably close to the real WOIO's first news in February 1995.

288. **Football fans in Cleveland** gave the Browns some of NFL's highest local TV ratings every week before the original franchise left town. The recent record was the telecast of their 1987 playoff game with the Denver Broncos, which registered a 62 rating, or 62 percent of all the homes in Greater Cleveland.

289. Venerable TV commentator **Dorothy Fuldheim** got a rude greeting at Solon High School in 1980 when two pranksters served her a vanilla cream pie in the face. The pranksters got 60 days in jail. Fuldheim's reaction: "I want them to serve every hour of the sentence. And if you could, send the lawyer to jail, too."

290. *Remember when* you didn't miss your favorite show when you and the family watched it while eating TV dinner off individual TV tables—metal trays clamped onto folding tubular metal legs? The first TV dinner—introduced by Swanson in 1954—included turkey, peas, sweet potatoes, corn-bread dressing, and gravy, and sold for 98 cents.

291. **Bob Uecker,** who played the play-by-play announcer for the worst-to-first place Indians in the "Major League" movies, showed fans that life really does imitate art when he joined Bob Costas and Joe Morgan on the NBC Sports team calling the 1995 World Series—the Tribe's first trip to the classic in 41 years.

292. **"The Cleveland Comedy Company"** was the local answer to *Saturday Night Live*, and ran as a series of occasional late-night weekend specials on Channel 5 starting in 1979. "Diamond Man" Larry Robinson was the first host, and music was by Kinsman Dazz, which later became the Dazz Band. The show ended after its driving force, disc jockey Bob James of WGAR-AM, left for California in 1981.

293. **Bob Dale** looked a bit like Jimmy Stewart and was one of Cleveland's first and most popular TV personalities. He lip-synched records and hosted the *Dinner Platter* show on WEWS from 1948 to 1956, and was an original co-host of the *1 O'Clock Club* in 1957 with Dorothy Fuldheim and Bill Gordon. He left Cleveland for San Diego, where he became a TV weatherman and contributor of light feature stories.

294. Jim Varney's rubber-faced **Ernest P. Worrell**, who always directed his comments at the unseen "Vern," was the local spokesman for Channel 61 in the early 1980s, just as he was starting a film career and becoming known nationally as a commercial pitchman for everything from banks to car dealerships. Know what I mean, Vern?

295. **Jim Finerty and Cathy Brugett** were original co-hosts of Channel 8's *PM Magazine*. A syndicated series with local features, it became the most successful show started in the late 1970s after the Federal Communications Commission tried to give local shows and syndicators a shot in the arm by moving the start of network "primetime" from 7:30 to 8 p.m.

296. **Winning Misses**: Beauty pageant contestants who say they want to get into broadcasting sometimes make it. Tana Carli, who won the hearts of viewers as TV-8's first female co-anchor from 1981 until 1983 on the 6 and 11 p.m. news, had already won favor as Miss Ohio. Robin Meade, hired as morning "update anchor" by TV-8 in 1993, was at the time the reigning Miss Ohio and a top-10 finalist in the 1992 Miss America Pageant. Gretchen Carlson, a weekend anchor on Channel 43 and later week night co-anchor with Denise Dufala on Channel 19, was Miss America of 1989. And lest anyone forget, one of the first receptionists at WEWS was Nancy Nesbitt, Miss Ohio of 1947, whom the station described somewhat breathlessly as "20, five feet five inches, 110 pounds, red hair, blue eyes, a student of song and dance."

297. **"Cash on the Line"** was the call-for-cash mid-day movie show hosted by Tom Haley on Channel 3 in the early 1960s. Its set featured a giant rotary-dial phone with the jackpot amount printed in the middle.

298. *Signature Saying:* Ron Penfound closed every show as Captain Penny saying, "You can fool some of the people all of the time, and all of the people some of the time, but you can't fool Mom. She's pretty nice and she's pretty smart—you listen to her and you won't go far wrong."

299. **"Uncle Bill's is for the People"** was the red-, white- and blue-themed commercial campaign used by the local discount chain in the Bicentennial-minded 1970s.

300. *Recollection: Gene Carroll.* *The Gene Carroll Show* started in 1948 on WEWS, proving so durable that it continued with other hosts after Carroll's death in 1972. He once described how important the amateur showcase was to its would-be performers: "We got anywhere from 20 to 100 acts [auditioning] a week. We weren't going to hold auditions the day President Kennedy was assassinated, but we had to keep the office open because some people may have been traveling to Cleveland from far away. That Friday was one of our biggest days."

301. *Remember when* Browns fans installed oversized home antennas or gathered in out-of-town motels to beat the 75-mile blackout on televised home games?

302. **Martin Savidge** was recognizable mainly for his distinctive deep voice after he moved from Channel 8 to CNN in 1996. The move involved more than getting to report from trouble spots around the globe—the anchor-reporter had to shave his moustache, trade his sneakers for $300 shoes, and spend a CNN clothing allowance on 11 new suits and 40 ties. All for someone, he ruefully noted, "who remembers standing on the Shoreway, freezing his butt off for a story."

303. *And now, a word from our sponsor:* "Straight Shootin'" Ed Stinn and "Big Hearted" Jim Connell stood back to back with six-guns, preparing to fight a duel, in commercials that shrewdly promoted their ostensibly feuding Chevy dealerships—Stinn's on the West Side and Connell's on the East Side. The portly Stinn wore a cowboy hat while the bespectacled Connell wore a Bat Masterson-style bowler.

304. Before *Polka Varieties*, Channel 5 brought viewers the bands and the music on **"The Old Dutch Polka Review,"** a Gene Carroll production sponsored by Old Dutch Beer.

305. Loud sport coats, usually plaid, matched his outspoken opinions and, along with his horn-rimmed glasses, served as trademarks of sportscaster **Gib Shanley** on Channel 5 and later Channel 43.

306. **The 10 o'clock news** returned to Cleveland in January 1988 on WUAB (Channel 43), anchored by Bob Hetherington and Romona Robinson. Gib Shanley was sports anchor and young Frank Cariello was meteorologist. The slogan: "The Time Is Right."

307. **Those Cleveland Jokes:** For more than a decade starting in the late 1960s, Cleveland was "consistently employed by network comics, game-show emcees and nightclub performers" as the butt of jokes—as was noted by *TV Guide* in a 1978 article titled, "Why Is Everybody Picking on Cleveland?" The jokes were irksome, but they were rooted in love: the Cleveland Clan, a colony of comedy writers and performers in Los Angeles, began writing and delivering them as evidence of affection for their hometown. One of them, actor Jack Riley, attributed the epidemic to *Laugh-In*—its staff needed a substitute for ethnic jokes, and knew that a joke had to be about somebody,

 something or some place. They decided to pick a funny city. Script supervisor Jack Hanrahan—who had worked for several Cleveland radio and TV stations, and the *Press*—mentioned an item in the paper about the Cuyahoga River catching fire. "A river on fire was a natural for laughs," Riley said. "Cleveland was unanimously voted as the city to get the treatment. But there was no malice. It was a fun thing."

308. **Pianist Ellie Frankel** and her trio backed up the host's singing and provided the music on *The Mike Douglas Show* during its years of production in Cleveland.

309. **"Dress and Guess,"** a game show, was one of the first programs on WEWS. Host Paul Hodges walked onstage in long underwear, donned distinctive articles of clothing, and a panel tried to guess which celebrity he was impersonating. The sponsor was Van Heusen Shirts.

Mike Douglas at Ellie Frankel's piano, 1962

Paul Hodges on "Dress and Guess"

Courtesy of Channel 5

310. *Remember when* Ghoulardi decorated a tree with mittens sent to him one Christmas season—and then set fire to the tree on the air when the holiday was over?

311. **Country music** was starting a surge in the early 1970s when "Dusty" Rogers hosted *The Roy Rogers Jr. Show* on Channel 5.

312. **Electric Avenue** tried to revive some of the spirit of *Upbeat* on Channel 8 in the post-disco era in 1988. Original MTV veejay and Lakewood native Nina Blackwood hosted the weekly dance series from Club Coconuts in the Flats. Seen Saturdays at dinnertime, it featured lip-synch performances from entertainers including Vanilla Ice, Tony! Toni! Tone!, and Lisa Lisa and the Cult Jam.

313. **Televangelist Rex Humbard**, of the Cathedral of Tomorrow in Cuyahoga Falls, broadcast a short daily show on Channel 8 that greeted early-rising youngsters waiting for *Captain Kangaroo*.

314. **Chippewa Lake Park** was the original home of Jungle Larry and the exotic animals he brought to Captain Penny's show, before Larry opened his "Safari Island" attraction at Cedar Point.

315. **"Red Goose Merry-Go-Round"** was the popular Saturday morning kids' show that ran from 1950–1955 on Channel 9 (and then Channel 8). Its host was curly-haired Walt "Kousin" Kay, who came from "Kousin Kay's Korner" on WJW radio. Coco the Clown and Merrily, the Lady from Story Land, were his sidekicks.

316. **Three Babes and a Bob** was Channel 5's weekend anchor team of the early 1990s. News anchors Liz Claman and Tonya Strong and weather forecaster Kerry O'Reilly famously competed for "face time" on camera while lone male Bob Stevens delivered sports.

317. **Neil Zurcher** began making his "One-Tank Trips" for Channel 8 in 1980, taking viewers to regional attractions in a tiny, distinctive vehicle—a red-and-white, two-passenger 1959 Nash Metropolitan.

Courtesy of Channel 8

318. **Monkeying Around:** Hoping to shake the famed imperturbability of sportscaster Jim Graner, a TV-3 news anchor led into his sportscast by reading, in wedding announcement style, a story about a zoo mating a male and female gorilla—and then asked, "What tune did they play for the wedding march, Jim?" Without hesitation, Graner replied, "That's easy—'Gorilla My Dreams.'"

319. **Barbra Streisand**, at the start of her career, was paid $1,000 to co-host a week of *The Mike Douglas Show*—five 90-minute shows—in the early 1960s. In one of local TV's famed miscalculations, the tapes were later erased for station editorials.

320. *And now, a word from our sponsor:* "I want to sell YOU . . . a car now." Crewcut Del Spitzer, flashing a broad, slightly gap-toothed smile that anticipated David Letterman by decades, always thrust a finger at the camera to emphasize "you" on his car commercials, which started running in the late 1950s. Besides giving him instant recognition, they made him the world's largest car dealer in the 1970s. Son Donnie, in matching crewcut, started appearing in the commercials when he was just nine, chirping, "My dad wants to sell YOU a car now."

321. **John Fitzgerald** sat at a bar delivering sports scores for Channel 8 on the *Carling Sports Final* in the 1950s.

322. *Remember when* you had to wait for the TV to warm up?

323. **"Hercules"** was the record by Ray Saporita that hit No. 14 on the national charts. Ray was a regular on *The Gene Carroll Show* from age 7 into adulthood.

324. **Sports Protest:** Outspoken Gib Shanley was sports anchor on Channel 5 when he surprised colleagues—and viewers—during the Iran hostage crisis by setting fire to an Iranian flag at the anchor desk during the late news, explaining it reflected his feelings about the situation.

325. Kids visiting **"Uncle Jake's House,"** the WEWS show hosted by Gene Carroll in the early 1950s, had to pretend they were descending into the basement on an elevator by bending their knees and dropping out of camera range.

Uncle Jake's House

326. **Alan Douglas** brought intensity, a richly
sonorous voice, and a professorial beard to his
brief role as original host of *The Morning
Exchange* in 1972. Once a producer and
announcer for WEWS and later an interviewer on
Channel 61, Douglas might be best remembered
as a droll and penetrating radio talk-show host in
the 1960s on WERE and WKYC (now WTAM).
Beset by personal problems that included the
death of his wife, he left *Morning Exchange* after

*Alan Douglas
and Jeanne Dixon*

less than eight months for a short-lived job at WNBC radio in New York.
Not long after, he took his own life at age 50 in his native Detroit.

327. *Signature Saying:* Leon Bibb, on Channel 3 and still on Channel 5, closed
programs with the words, "Good luck, be well, we'll talk again."

328. Presenting **anchor teams** that paired a man and a woman, instead of two men, became standard practice for Cleveland TV after Tana Carli joined Tim Taylor on WJW and helped *Newscenter 8* become the city's top-rated newscast. Carli was already known to viewers not as a reporter, but as an accordion-playing former Miss Ohio and runner-up for Miss America.

329. **Feagler's Start:** TV made Dick Feagler as famous for his rubber-faced, eyebrow-wagging mugging as for his careful writing and informed opinions. He was a *Cleveland Press* columnist when he delivered his first commentary on Channel 3 in 1974, as one of a number of print reporters who found temporary work on TV during a newspaper strike. But Feagler stayed after the strike ended, getting a weekly interview show in 1979 and even serving a brief, unhappy stint as a Channel 3 News anchor in the early '90s.

330. **Happier Ending:** Clevelanders all knew that *The Fugitive*, starring David Janssen as a doctor wrongly convicted of his wife's murder, was inspired by the Sam Sheppard case. Many even confused the show's "one-armed man" with the case's "bushy-haired intruder." Fiction had a happier ending than reality: Janssen's Dr. Richard Kimble was exonerated after the one-armed man was found and plunged to his death from a tower in the show's August 1967 finale, which stood for about a decade as the highest-rated series episode of the modern era.

331. Dance instructor **Dick Blake,** sporting a blond pompadour, was the original choreographer of *The Big Five Show*. After the show's name changed to *Upbeat*, Jeff Kutash assumed the choreography duties. He eventually went on to Las Vegas.

332. **Buckeyes, Real and Imagined**: *The Drew Carey Show*, *3rd Rock from the Sun*, and *Homefront* are all set in Northeast Ohio. And these network shows were also set in the Buckeye State: NBC's *Family Ties* (Columbus), NBC's *Harper Valley PTA* (fictitious Harper Valley, Ohio), NBC's short-lived *It's A Man's World* (houseboat on Ohio River), CBS's *WKRP in Cincinnati* and the syndicated *Mary Hartman, Mary Hartman* and *Fernwood 2-Night* (both set in fictitious Fernwood in central Ohio).

333. **"Now you see it, now you don't"** described the early years of public station WVIZ. Its week-night evening schedule was so limited that it was printed apart from the regular TV-listing grids in *The Plain Dealer* and the *Cleveland Press*, and its weekend programming consisted of only a few hours on Sunday night. That changed after the station's first March membership drive, in 1971, which was billed as "SOS" because it aimed to finance "Sesame [Street] on Saturday."

334. **Jack Reynolds** was best known for his rich voice as an announcer for two decades at Channel 43—where he was indelibly associated with pro wrestling shows from 1969 to 1976—and on radio stations including WHK, 3WE, and WQAL. He hit the big screen in 1974 in the wedding scene of *The Godfather*, playing an Army captain sitting at a table with old friend Michael Corleone (Al Pacino). Ironically, his voice isn't heard: His line—"We haven't had this much fun since the Blitzkrieg"—was among those cut.

335. **Hi-ho, Steverino:** NBC's *Tonight* show ran on ABC affiliate WEWS when Johnny Carson took over as host in 1962. The NBC affiliate, KYW, preferred a new show starring Steve Allen—"*Tonight's* original host"—that was being syndicated by Westinghouse, which just happened to own KYW.

336. **"Stay smoochie ... you rascal, you"** was the signature sign-off of Bill "Smoochie" Gordon, the gregarious, lip-locking deejay from WHR radio who joined the *1 O'Clock Club* show. Best known as the teasing partner of Dorothy Fuldheim, the one-time blues spinner was the only *1 O'Clock Club* host to appear during its entire run from 1957-64.

Dorothy Fuldheim and Bill "Smoochie" Gordon, 1957

337. **Professor Yul Flunk** wore a mortarboard and academic robes when he showed up on *Captain Penny's Fun House* to dispense cock-eyed knowledge and serious advice. He was really producer-director Jim Breslin.

338. **"Adventure Road"** was the much loved and often parodied series hosted by Jim Doney on Channel 8 from December 1962 to May 1975. Guests

brought travel films and shared details of their trips with Doney, an announcer and newscaster, whose show was "a carbon copy of the program George Pierrot pioneered in Detroit." Both shows were canceled the same month because, Doney said, "Travelogs traditionally draw older audiences and advertisers have very little regard for anyone over 35."

339. **Cleveland TV got a new look in 1955**, when NBC realized its hope to get into a bigger market by making a deal to swap WNBK and its Cleveland operations with Westinghouse in Philadelphia. WNBK became KYW for the next decade, until the Federal Communications Commission overturned the deal, concluding that NBC had forced Westinghouse into the agreement. NBC returned to Cleveland, and well-regarded KYW became WKYC, which was tainted for years by the image of reluctant, "carpet-bagging" ownership.

340. **Jack Corrigan**, who was only in his 30s when he started broadcasting Tribe games on Channel 43, won the nickname "Gramps" from some fans for following the practice of referring to rookies, regardless of age, as "the youngster."

341. **Herb Score**, loved for both his personality and occasional Herb-isms ("And the score is Cleveland 3–Indians 2!"), called Tribe games on TV from 1964 to 1966. He moved to radio in 1967 as successor to the legendary Jimmy Dudley and remained until his retirement in 1997.

342. **Bernie Kosar** made his sitcom debut on the "Drewstock" episode of *The Drew Carey Show* in February 1997, walking into Drew's garage and saying he was looking for the bathroom. Drew, eager to accommodate the Browns star, said he could use the garage—as long as he didn't have to "take a Modell." Mayor Michael White also had a speaking part in the episode, and Cleveland's Joe Walsh, of the James Gang and the Eagles, performed with Little Richard.

343. **Why We Loved Al:** *Action 3 News* anchor Doug Adair once recounted for viewers that he had experienced a minor street assault with a rolled-up newspaper, telling anchor desk colleague Al Roker that his attacker was one of "your people." Without missing a beat, Roker responded in mock astonishment, "You got mugged by a weatherman?"

344. **Herb Kamm** was the gregarious, gossip-writing editor of the *Cleveland Press* in the 1970s who hosted a weekly interview show, *Kamm's Corner*, on Channel 25.

345. **"The Quarterback Club"** was the weekly highlights show hosted at dinnertime from a den-like set on Channel 5 by Browns announcer Ken Coleman in the 1960s. National City Bank and Fisher Foods were the sponsors.

346. **GRrfield 1-2323** is the phone number Clevelanders know as well as their own and can sing as well as "Happy Birthday." Endlessly repeated in commercials that once featured Indians announcer Jimmy Dudley, the number was for the Aluminum Siding Corporation—now the Home Corporation, since aluminum siding has given way to vinyl siding in most places.

347. **Dave C and the Sharptones** were the house band on Channel 5's *Big Five Show*. When the show went national and changed its name to *Upbeat*, they changed the theme song lyrics from (in their entirety) "Let's all go to the *Big Five Show*" to "Let's all go to the *Upbeat* show."

348. *Remember when* the TV repairman visiting your house would take a big mirror off the wall and set it up so he could see the picture on the set while he was working in the back? The scariest words you could hear came from behind the set: "Looks like I've got to take it to the shop."

349. **"The Afternoon Exchange"** was the 5 p.m. companion program to *The Morning Exchange* that debuted on January 30, 1978, hosted by Wilma Smith with Joel Rose and later Don Webster and Steve Wolford. It was renamed *Live on Five* in 1981 and became more news-oriented as an attempt to fill some of the void left by the closing of the *Cleveland Press*.

350. **The Watergate Hearings** were held during business hours, but they kept thousands of Clevelanders glued to the screen when they were rebroadcast nightly on Channel 25 in prime time during the summer of 1973.

351. **Barnaby's Beginning:** Linn Sheldon was playing Og, the leprechaun from *Finian's Rainbow*, as part of his night club routine at the old Alpine Village on Playhouse Square, when a director from Channel 3 asked if he could adapt it for a TV kids show in 1957. Sheldon did, using the same pointy ears and makeup, but mentioned to a stage-hand at the first show that the new character didn't have a name. The stagehand said, "My dog's name is Barnaby." Sheldon said, "That's good enough for me." He retired as Barnaby in January 1990.

352. **Rich Little** ticked off Clevelanders during his televised performance at Ronald Reagan's 1981 inaugural gala. "Do you know how to keep the Russians out of Poland?" Little asked. "Change the name to Cleveland." That joke earned him the ire of U.S. Rep. Mary Rose Oakar, who refused to shake his hand, and he got some 15,000 com-plaining letters. After apologizing a month later on *The Tonight Show* and offering to do a show in Cleveland, he played the Front Row Theatre in Highland Heights in May 1982. Still apologizing, he said he'd changed the punch line from Cleveland to Buffalo.

353. The sight of short pants on a grown man on TV—indeed, a six-foot-three man—disturbed some adults watching **Franz the Toymaker** in 1964. Not only that, said Franz (Ray Stawiarski), but one took his on-air German accent too seriously. "A lady called the station to demand they take that foreigner off the program and give the job to a good American," he said.

354. ABC's **"Monday Night Football"** earned the lasting enmity of Cleveland fans by not showing the anti-Art Modell banners during the Browns' final *Monday Night Football* appearance for four years on November 13, 1995 in Pittsburgh. Plus, the Browns lost to the Steelers, 20–3.

355. *Remember when* add-on gadgets adorned TV sets? Among them were giant magnifying glasses that increased the picture size from tiny screens, and spinning wheels that were set up in front of sets to create a "color" picture.

356. **Boot in Mouth:** Channel 3 sports anchor Wayland Boot was a brief sensation in the mid-1980s with his folksy style and blues-accompanied "Old Blue Scoreboard." His star faded when fans began to question his sports savvy—and learned of an interview in his former hometown of Portland, Oregon, where he said "The move from Portland to Cleveland was like turning in a Ferrari for a dump truck." Boot added, "Clean air, clean government, that's what I miss . . . I'm not really a Cleveland fan. I love when the Steelers come here and kick the Browns' fannies."

357. **Brookpark Road** was officially renamed "Sesame Street" for WVIZ's 25th anniversary in February 1990. There were even traffic reports updating commuters about conditions on Sesame Street that day.

358. *Recollection: Don Webster.* Don Webster came to Cleveland and WEWS in 1964 to do *The Big Five Show* (later retitled *Upbeat*), and *Quick as a Wink*, a game show that lasted just 13 weeks against *The Mike Douglas Show* on KYW. He later hosted *It's Academic*, Ohio Lottery shows and *Afternoon Exchange*, served as station manager, and became one of the city's most popular weather forecasters. But he feared for his future when he was asked to take over *The Gene Carroll Show* after the the passing of its original host and the untimely cancer deaths of two replacements, Ron Penfound and Jim Runyon. "They said, 'Webster, it's yours,'" he recalled. "I said, 'Wait a minute, I'm feeling pretty good, I'm not sure I want to do this.' So then I took it over and they had a pool at the station to see how long I was going to last. Fortunately, the show died before I did."

359. **The Baseball Network** was a brief and disastrous experiment by NBC, ABC, and Major League Baseball that bounced the 1995 Cleveland-Atlanta World Series between two networks. Viewers ended up with a dizzying array of announcer combinations in the Playoffs and Series that included Jim Palmer, Al Michaels, Tim McCarver, Bob Costas, Bob Uecker, Steve Zabriskie, Tommy Hutton, Brent Musburger, and Jim Kaat.

360. **Warren Guthrie** was the "Sohio Reporter" on Channel 8 until 1963, and one of Cleveland's best known anchors in the 1950s. A speech professor at Western Reserve University, he was noted for shunning scripts in favor of delivering the news from memory with the aid of index cards.

Warren Guthrie (left) and executives, 1952

361. **Shock Theater** was the Friday night horror movie show that debuted on Channel 8 on January 18, 1963. Within weeks, it was a runaway hit better known simply as *Ghoulardi*, for its irreverent, post-beatnik host, played by announcer and commercial spokesman Ernie Anderson. It lasted until Anderson decided to pack up for Hollywood late in 1966.

362. **John and Janet** were the polka-loving, Cheez-Whiz-eating characters played by Ernie Anderson and Gena Hallaman on "Parma Place," the *Peyton Place* parody that ran for 11 episodes in early 1966 on Anderson's *Ghoulardi* show. John worked by day at an ad agency and by night as a "muckraker" on a barge on Lake Erie.

363. **Doug and Mona** became a hot item and Cleveland's first and only husband-and-wife anchor team on Channel 3 in the late 1970s after Mona Scott, a weather forecaster-turned-news anchor, married Doug Adair. His previous on-air partners, during 25 years at Channel 3 and Channel 8, included Ken Armstrong, Roger Goodrich, Joel Daly, Marty Ross, and Virgil Dominic. The couple moved to Columbus TV in 1983.

Joel Daly and Doug Adair

364. **Bill Jacocks** made an impression on viewers with a voice so deep it could shake floors and square-jawed good looks. But he also had the distinction of being Cleveland's first full-time African-American anchor, handling weekend evening newscasts on Channel 5 at the start of the 1970s.

Courtesy of Channel 5

365. **Lion Untaming:** Animal stories don't always make cute pictures. In October 1976, WKYC (Channel 3) reporter Del Donahoo received 48 stitches after being mauled by a declawed lion named Fester in front of a rolling camera and about 250 people at the Midway Mall in Elyria. Resulting worldwide publicity included a front page photo in a newspaper in New Delhi. "All part of a day's work," said Donahoo, who suffered no lasting damage. "It gave me some identity in a way most people won't forget, though I could have won the Mr. Stupid award."